# DARINA ALLEN
## SIMPLY DELICIOUS
### The Classic Collection

# DARINA ALLEN
## SIMPLY DELICIOUS
## The Classic Collection

100 timeless, tried & tested recipes

Photography by Peter Cassidy

**Kyle Books**

*To the memory of Myrtle Allen, my lifelong inspiration*

An Hachette UK Company
www.hachette.co.uk

This edition published in 2019, first published in Great Britain in 2018 by
Kyle Books, an imprint of Kyle Cathie Ltd
Carmelite House, 50 Victoria Embankment, London EC4Y 0DZ
www.kylebooks.co.uk

ISBN: 978 0 857835 550

Distributed in the US by Hachette Book Group, 1290 Avenue of the Americas,
4th and 5th Floors, New York, NY 10104

Distributed in Canada by Canadian Manda Group, 664 Annette St., Toronto,
Ontario, Canada M6S 2C8

Publisher: Joanna Copestick
Editor: Vicky Orchard
Design: Jane Humphrey
Photography: Peter Cassidy
Food styling: Lizzie Harris
Props styling: Agathe Gits
Production: Nic Jones and Gemma John

Printed and bound in China

10 9 8 7 6 5 4 3 2 1

**RECIPE SYMBOLS**

❄ Freezes perfectly for
2 to 3 months but use
sooner rather than later.

# contents

# Introduction

Early in 1987, "a knock came to the door" as we say in Ireland, and the letter carrier delivered a letter that in some ways was to change the course of the rest of my life. It was from the Controller of Programmes at RTÉ, our national television station, and contained a proposal to Myrtle Allen and me for a pilot for a cookery series. It was terrifically exciting, tempting in many ways, but also beyond scary… I had never seen a television camera in my life and had absolutely no idea how to go about making a television program. I tossed the proposal backward and forward in my head, scared I would make a total fool of myself, yet excited at the prospect. After much toing and froing I decided it would be easier to live with the series not being a huge success than with the eternal question of "What if…?"

We filmed the pilot in August 1987 and RTÉ commissioned the first series in July 1988, to be filmed that September. The original plan was to publish the recipes in the weekly RTÉ Guide, but I was worried that we would have endless phone calls when people mislaid it. So, despite having no idea how to go about writing a cookbook either, I proposed that I do just that. The producer Colette Farmer was concerned that there wouldn't be enough recipes, but the Ballymaloe Cookery School had been operating since 1983, so we already had a growing repertoire of dishes—no problem there then. Gill & Macmillan agreed to publish the cookbook in paperback, but what to call it…The name Darina Allen meant nothing at that time, so after much discussion with the crew, *Simply Delicious* was proposed. Apparently, I had repeated these two words regularly and it seemed to reflect the food that I loved to cook and was so anxious to share— how easy it was to make simple and delicious food with beautiful, fresh local produce.

The first program was to be aired on Monday 13 March 1989 at 8 p.m. My director Colette Farmer was also production assistant and later a producer of the *Late Late Show*, and was famous in her own right as the face behind the command "Roll it there Colette," when Gay Byrne would show a previously recorded piece during an interview. She understandably had Gay's ear, so he agreed to have me on as a guest on his Saturday night show. I was never so terrified before or since, but survived. Gay could be unpredictable, even provocative, but he introduced me enthusiastically to the Irish people and I was launched.

After the first few programs, people poured into the shops to buy the little 78-page *Simply Delicious* paperback. For many, it was the first cookbook they ever owned, the recipes well-tested for the Ballymaloe Cookery School worked, so as the Gill & Macmillan representative put it one night after a book signing, the book was selling in "telephone numbers" and shops quickly ran out of copies. It went into a second printing immediately and there was a paper shortage, so for several of the eight weeks the program was on air there wasn't a copy of *Simply Delicious* to be had in the country. Furthermore, the success was fueled by another unlikely element. RTÉ did not anticipate the appeal of this new cookery series and ran it opposite Britain's favorite soap opera *Coronation Street*. This was at a time when most houses would have been proud to own just one television and long before any form of playback, so there was many a family "fracas" about which program to watch. Viewers wrote to RTÉ and rang into chat shows to complain that it was causing "strife" within the family. The repeat was rescheduled...

*Simply Delicious* went on to make Irish publishing history, topping the best sellers for months in a row and selling more copies than any previously published cookbook in Ireland: 115,000 copies in the first year of publication. I went on to do an additional six *Simply Delicious* books to accompany a series of the same name.

I've often been told that "dog-eared" copies of these books are treasured possessions in many households and have in many cases been passed on to the next generation. Since then I've gone on to publish sixteen more cookbooks. The *Simply Delicious* books have been out of print for many years, but people regularly ask where they can find a copy of one or another, so I'm delighted to be republishing this collection of 100 classic recipes from *Simply Delicious 1* and *2* and *Simply Delicious Vegetables*.

Choosing the recipes was a fascinating experience—so many have stood the test of time and are still perennial favorites. Some we have tweaked over the past thirty years or added more contemporary garnishes or complementary spices as the range of ingredients available has expanded considerably in the time since the recipes were first published.

Many of our happiest childhood memories are connected to food. I hope you will enjoy this selection of recipes. For me it's such a joy to know that for many, these simply delicious dishes have become treasured favorites to share with family and friends around the table. And I'm hoping that many of these time-honored recipes will still be relished and enjoyed in thirty years' time...

# soups & appetizers

# WINTER CELERY SOUP

## with Cashel Blue & toasted hazelnuts

Celery gets a bad rap, but at Ballymaloe we cook it in lots of exciting ways—I love this wintery soup, light and delicious garnished with creamy crumbly blue cheese and some toasted hazelnuts.

1¼ pounds celery, finely chopped

3 tablespoons salted butter

5 ounces potatoes, peeled and cut into ¼-inch dice

5 ounces onions, peeled and chopped

3½ cups homemade chicken stock

⅔ cup to 1¼ cups creamy milk

sea salt and freshly ground black pepper

*For the garnish*

a few tablespoons whipped cream

2 tablespoons blue cheese, preferably Irish Cashel Blue or Crozier Blue cheese, crumbled

2 tablespoons hazelnuts, skinned, toasted, and coarsely chopped

chervil or flat-leaf parsley sprigs

Using a vegetable peeler, remove the strings from the outside stalks of the celery and reserve to use in stock.

In a heavy-bottom saucepan, melt the butter. When it foams, add the potatoes, onions, and celery, and toss in the butter until evenly coated. Season with salt and freshly ground pepper. Cover with a wax paper lid (to keep in the steam) and the pan lid and sweat over gentle heat until the vegetables are soft but not colored, about 10 minutes. Add the chicken stock and simmer until the celery is fully cooked, 10 to 12 minutes.

Using a blender or food processor, blend the soup until smooth, adding the creamy milk to taste and to thin to the required consistency. Season to taste.

Serve the soup piping hot with a spoonful of whipped cream on top. Sprinkle with the crumbled blue cheese, coarsely chopped hazelnuts, and chervil or flat-leaf parsley sprigs.

### VARIATION

*For a vegetarian version* substitute vegetable stock for the chicken stock and for a vegan option use extra virgin olive oil instead of butter and omit the milk, cream, and cheese.

# WATERCRESS SOUP

This soup has been a favorite on the menu at Ballymaloe House since it opened in 1964. Watercress contains large amounts of vitamins K, C, and A, and some vitamins E and B6. It also contains iron, calcium, manganese, potassium, thiamine, magnesium, and phosphorus, and is a valuable source of nutrients. Wild watercress has more depth of flavor than the cultivated version, so see if you can find some to use in this recipe.

3 tablespoons salted butter

5 ounces potatoes, peeled and chopped

4 ounces onions, peeled and chopped

3¾ cups homemade chicken stock, vegetable stock, or water, boiling

1¼ cups creamy milk, boiling

8 ounces watercress, coarse stems removed and chopped

sea salt and freshly ground black pepper

In a heavy-bottom saucepan, melt the butter. When it foams, add the potatoes and onions and toss them until well coated. Sprinkle with salt and freshly ground pepper. Cover with a wax paper lid and the lid of the pan and sweat over gentle heat for 10 minutes.

When the vegetables are almost soft but not colored, add the boiling stock or water and milk. (It is essential to boil the stock and milk before adding, otherwise the enzymes in the watercress may cause the milk to curdle.)

Return to a boil and cook until the potatoes and onions are fully cooked. Add the freshly chopped watercress, return to a boil, and cook with the lid off until the watercress is just cooked, 4 to 5 minutes. Be careful not to overcook the soup or it will lose its fresh green color. Serve as is or blend the soup in a blender or food processor until smooth. Season to taste.

### VARIATION

*For a vegetarian version* use vegetable stock, and for a vegan version substitute extra virgin olive oil for the butter and use extra vegetable stock instead of milk.

# MUSHROOM SOUP

Serves 8 to 9

This is a super-quick soup to make and best using portobello mushrooms, as they have so much more flavor than the button variety. You can also substitute meadow mushrooms, *Agaricus campestris*, in season. Give them a quick wash under the faucet. Trim the roots if necessary, though it's better to leave the roots in the ground if you are foraging yourself.

The soup base of this recipe (without the stock) is a great way to preserve a glut of meadow mushrooms. It freezes perfectly for several months. To use, just thaw, add the stock and milk, and then bring to a boil for 3 to 4 minutes. Season to taste before serving.

3 tablespoons salted butter

4 ounces onions, peeled and finely chopped

1 pound portobello mushrooms

3 tablespoons all-purpose flour

2½ cups homemade chicken stock, boiling

2½ cups whole milk, boiling

dash of light cream (optional)

sea salt and freshly ground black pepper

thyme sprigs, to garnish

In a saucepan, melt the butter over gentle heat. Toss the onions in it, cover with a wax paper lid, and let sweat until soft and fully cooked.

Meanwhile, chop the mushrooms very finely. It's best to hand chop the mushrooms, but if you do not have time to chop them very finely, just slice them and then pulse the cooked soup in a food processor or blender for a second or two. Be careful not to overdo it, as the soup should be chunky.

Add the mushrooms to the pan and cook over high heat for 5 to 6 minutes. Now stir in the flour, cook over low heat for 2 to 3 minutes, and season with salt and freshly ground pepper.

Add the boiling stock and milk gradually, stirring continuously. Increase the heat and bring to a boil. Taste and add a dash of cream to enrich if necessary. Serve immediately or reheat later, garnished with thyme sprigs.

### VARIATION

*For a vegetarian version* substitute vegetable stock for the chicken stock, and for a vegan version use extra virgin olive oil to replace the butter. Instead of milk and cream, use all stock or substitute soy or almond milk.

# ONION & THYME LEAF SOUP

Serves 6

This silky, flavorsome soup is so much more than the sum of its parts. Serve it in one of two ways, depending on your mood. You may want to blend it to a smooth texture or just ladle it directly into a wide soup bowl with all the chunky bits intact. It's irresistible scattered with fresh thyme leaves and flowers in season.

3 tablespoons salted butter

1 pound onions, peeled and chopped

8 ounces potatoes, peeled and chopped

2 teaspoons thyme leaves

4¼ cups homemade chicken or vegetable stock,
    boiling

⅔ cup light cream or creamy milk, or to taste

sea salt and freshly ground black pepper

softly whipped cream (optional), to garnish

thyme leaves and thyme or chive flowers,
    to garnish

In a heavy-bottom saucepan, melt the butter. As soon as it foams, add the onions and potatoes and stir until they are well coated with butter. Add the thyme leaves and season with salt and freshly ground pepper. Cover with a wax paper lid and the lid of the pan and let sweat over low heat until the potatoes and onions are soft but not colored, about 10 minutes. Add the boiling stock and bring to a boil, then simmer until the onions and potatoes are cooked, 5 to 8 minutes.

Using a blender or food processor, blend the soup until smooth and then add the cream or creamy milk to taste. Season to taste.

Serve in soup bowls or in a soup tureen garnished with a spoonful of softly whipped cream, if desired. Sprinkle with thyme leaves and thyme or chive flowers to garnish.

## VARIATION

*For a vegetarian version* substitute vegetable stock for the chicken stock, and for a vegan option use extra virgin olive oil instead of butter and omit the cream and milk.

# SPRING CABBAGE SOUP

Serves 6

It doesn't seem to occur to many people to use cabbage for soup, yet of all the soups I make, the flavor of cabbage soup surprises most—it is unexpectedly delicious. I use Greyhound or pointed cabbage, but crinkly Savoy works brilliantly later in the year.

3½ tablespoons salted butter

4 ounces onions, peeled and chopped

4½ ounces potatoes, peeled and diced

3½ cups homemade light chicken stock, boiling

9 ounces spring cabbage leaves, stems removed, shredded, and chopped

¼ to ½ cup light cream or creamy milk

sea salt and freshly ground black pepper

crumbled cured Spanish chorizo or
    Gremolata (page 84), to garnish (optional)

In a heavy-bottom saucepan, melt the butter. When it foams, add the onions and potatoes and toss them in the butter until well coated. Sprinkle with salt and freshly ground pepper. Cover with a wax paper lid and the lid of the pan and let sweat over gentle heat until soft but not colored, about 10 minutes. Add the boiling stock and boil until the potatoes are tender. Add the cabbage and cook, uncovered, until the cabbage is just cooked, 4 to 5 minutes. Keep the lid off to preserve the bright green color. Do not overcook or the vegetables will lose both their fresh flavor and color.

Using a blender or food processor, blend the soup until smooth. Season to taste. Add the cream or creamy milk before serving. Serve on its own or with a sprinkling of crumbled cured Spanish chorizo or gremolata over the top, if desired.

### VARIATION

*For a vegetarian version* substitute vegetable stock for the chicken stock and use the gremolata instead of the crumbled chorizo to garnish. For a vegan option, use extra virgin olive oil instead of butter and omit the cream or creamy milk.

# VINE-RIPENED TOMATO & SPEARMINT SOUP

Serves 5

Tomato soup is to soup what apple tart is to desserts—top of the list of all-time favorites. The marvelous thing about this recipe is that you can easily vary it in so many different ways, making it almost seem like a different soup each time. It's best to use a tomato puree made from vine-ripened tomatoes in season. However, good-quality canned tomatoes also produce a really good result, but because they are rather more acidic than fresh tomatoes, you need lots more sugar.

There are many varieties of mint in the herb garden, but spearmint is the most versatile and has the cleanest, freshest taste. Try to find the type that has shiny rather than furry leaves. Basil or cilantro can also be substituted for spearmint with delicious results.

1 tablespoon salted butter

4 ounces onions, peeled and finely chopped

3¼ cups Tomato Puree (see right)

   or 2 (14½-ounce) cans diced tomatoes,
    pureed and strained

1 cup Béchamel Sauce (page 116)

1 cup homemade chicken or vegetable stock

2 tablespoons freshly chopped spearmint,
   plus leaves to garnish

1 to 2 tablespoons or pinch of granulated sugar

½ cup light cream (optional)

softly whipped cream, to garnish

sea salt and freshly ground black pepper

*For the tomato puree*

2 pounds very ripe tomatoes

1 small onion, peeled and chopped

good pinch of granulated sugar

good pinch of salt

a few twists of black pepper

Make the tomato puree, if using: Cut the tomatoes into quarters and put into a stainless steel saucepan with the onion, sugar, salt, and freshly ground pepper. Cook over gentle heat until the tomatoes are soft (no water is needed). Pass through the fine blade of a mouli food mill or a nylon strainer. Let cool completely, then chill or freeze.

In a medium-size saucepan, melt the butter over gentle heat. When it foams, add the onions, toss, and cover with a wax paper lid and the lid of the pan. Cook until soft but not colored, 5 to 6 minutes. Add the homemade tomato puree or the pureed, strained canned tomatoes, the béchamel sauce, and stock. Bring to a boil, add the chopped mint, and season with salt, freshly ground pepper, and the larger quantity of sugar if you are using canned tomatoes, otherwise just a pinch. Bring to a boil and then simmer for a few minutes. Using a blender or food processor, blend the soup until smooth. Taste and add more stock to dilute if necessary.

Return to a boil, season to taste, and serve with the addition of the light cream if desired. Garnish with a swirl of whipped cream and some spearmint leaves. Like most soups, this one can be refrigerated for 3 to 4 days and it reheats very well.

# WINTER LEEK & POTATO SOUP

The classic winter soup loved by everyone, from tiny tots to elders. Once again this soup can be served either with the chunks of vegetables intact or pureed. A tablespoon of finely sliced buttered leeks served in the center of this soup makes a more substantial version.

3½ tablespoons salted butter

1 pound potatoes, peeled and cut into ¼-inch dice

4 ounces onions, peeled and cut into ¼-inch dice

1 pound white parts of leeks, finely sliced
(reserve the green tops for another soup or
vegetable stock)

3½ to 5 cups light homemade chicken stock,
boiling

⅓ cup plus 1 tablespoon heavy whipping cream,
or to taste, plus more to garnish

⅔ cup whole milk, or to taste

sea salt and freshly ground black pepper

finely chopped chives, to garnish

In a heavy-bottom saucepan, melt the butter. When it foams, add the potatoes, onions, and leeks, and turn them in the butter until well coated. Season well, sprinkle with salt and freshly ground pepper, and toss again. Cover with a wax paper lid and the pan lid. Let sweat over gentle heat until the vegetables are soft but not colored, about 10 minutes.

Add 3½ cups of boiling chicken stock, return to a boil, and then simmer until the vegetables are just cooked. Do not overcook or the soup will lose its fresh flavor.

Using a blender or food processor, blend the soup until smooth and silky. Taste and adjust the seasoning, if necessary. Add the cream and milk to taste. You may need to add the extra stock if you prefer a thinner soup. Garnish with a swirl of cream and some finely chopped chives.

### VARIATIONS

*Green Leek & Potato Soup* Use the green parts of the leeks as well as the more delicate blanched root ends. The soup will have a stronger flavor but will also be super delicious.

*Vichyssoise* Serve chilled in small bowls with extra cream and a sprinkling of chives and a few chive flowers sprinkled over the top in season.

*For a vegetarian version* substitute vegetable stock for the chicken stock, and for a vegan option use extra virgin olive oil instead of the butter and omit the cream and milk.

# RUTABAGA & BACON SOUP with parsley oil

Serves 6 to 8

I love rutabaga, an inexpensive, super-versatile vegetable with lots of flavor and one that's often forgotten. This soup is an example of how it can sing. A bit of diced cured Spanish chorizo or crumbled and mixed with chopped parsley is also delicious sprinkled on top.

1 tablespoon sunflower oil

5 ounces rindless bacon, cut into ½-inch dice

4 ounces onions, peeled and chopped

4 ounces potatoes, peeled and diced

12 ounces rutabaga, peeled and cut into
   ⅓-inch dice

3¾ cups homemade chicken stock

light cream or creamy milk, to taste

sea salt and freshly ground black pepper

*For the parsley oil*

1 cup freshly chopped flat-leaf parsley

3½ tablespoons extra virgin olive oil

*For the garnish*

freshly ground black pepper

sautéed diced bacon

croutons

First make the parsley oil: In a blender, blend the parsley with the extra virgin olive oil until smooth and green.

Next make the soup: In a saucepan, heat the oil, add the bacon, and cook over gentle heat until crisp and golden. Using a slotted spoon, remove to a plate and set aside.

Toss the onions, potatoes, and rutabaga in the oil in the pan. Season with salt and freshly ground pepper. Cover with a wax paper lid to keep in the steam and sweat over gentle heat until soft but not colored, about 10 minutes. Add the stock and bring to a boil, then simmer until the vegetables are fully cooked, 10 to 15 minutes. Using the blender or a food processor, blend the soup until smooth. Taste and add a bit of cream or creamy milk and some extra seasoning if necessary.

Serve with a drizzle of parsley oil, a grind of black pepper, and a mixture of crispy bacon and croutons sprinkled on top.

### VARIATION

*For a vegetarian version* use vegetable stock instead of chicken stock and omit the bacon. For a vegan option, omit the cream or creamy milk as well.

# GREEN PEA SOUP with fresh mint cream

Serves 6 to 8

This soup has the quintessential flavor of summer. If you can get beautiful fresh green peas, use the pods to make a vegetable stock as a basis for the soup. Having said that, best-quality frozen peas also make a delicious soup. Either way, be careful not to overcook.

This soup may also be served chilled in smaller portions. It can be enjoyed unblended but the flavor is more intense when pureed. To serve, put a few fresh peas and pea shoots into wide soup bowls. Put the soup into a pitcher—each guest then pours the soup into their bowl themselves.

1 ounce bacon or lean ham

1 tablespoon salted butter

2 scallions, green and white parts, chopped

outside leaves of 1 head lettuce, shredded

1 mint sprig, plus freshly chopped mint to garnish

5 cups light homemade chicken or
   vegetable stock or water, boiling

pinch of granulated sugar

1½ pounds fresh or frozen green peas

2 tablespoons heavy whipping cream, or to taste

sea salt and freshly ground black pepper

whipped cream, to garnish

Cut the bacon or ham into very fine shreds. In a saucepan, melt the butter and sweat the bacon or ham for about 5 minutes. Add the scallions and cook for another 1 to 2 minutes. Next add the lettuce, mint sprig, and boiling stock or water. Season with the sugar, salt, and pepper. Return to a boil with the lid off, add the peas, and cook until they are just tender, 3 to 4 minutes.

Using a blender or food processor, blend the soup until smooth and add the whipping cream to taste. Serve hot or chilled garnished with a spoonful of whipped cream and some freshly chopped mint.

If this soup is made ahead, reheat uncovered and serve immediately. It will lose its fresh taste and bright lively color if it sits in a bain-marie or simmers at length in a pot.

## VARIATIONS

Pea & Bacon or Chorizo Soup  Add a few tiny crispy bacon or cured Spanish chorizo pieces as a garnish.

For a vegetarian version  use vegetable stock and omit the bacon, ham, or chorizo. For a vegan version, use extra virgin olive oil instead of butter and omit the cream too.

# POTATO & FRESH HERB SOUP

Serves 6

Most people have potatoes and onions in the house even if the pantry is otherwise bare, so can make this simply delicious soup at a moment's notice. While the vegetables are sweating, pop a few white soda scones or Cheddar cheese scones into the oven to really impress your family and friends. I sometimes omit the fresh herbs and drizzle the soup with parsley or arugula pesto. Some buttered cabbage or kale stirred in before serving turns it into colcannon soup, while crispy bacon or cured Spanish chorizo pieces and flat-leaf parsley sprigs transform an everyday potato soup into a "cheffier" version.

4 tablespoons salted butter

15 ounces potatoes, peeled and cut into 3-inch dice

4 ounces onions, peeled and cut into 3-inch dice

1 teaspoon salt

a few grinds of freshly ground black pepper

1 to 2 tablespoons in total of the following fresh herbs—parsley, thyme, lemon balm, and chives

3¾ cups homemade chicken or vegetable stock, boiling

about ½ cup creamy milk

freshly chopped herbs and chive or thyme flowers in season

In a heavy-bottom saucepan, melt the butter. When it foams, add the potatoes and onions and toss them in the butter until well coated. Sprinkle with the salt and pepper. Cover with a wax paper lid and the lid of the pan. Sweat over gentle heat for about 10 minutes.

When the vegetables are soft but not colored, add the freshly chopped herbs and boiling stock and continue to cook until the vegetables are soft, 3 to 4 minutes.

Using a blender or food processor, blend the soup until smooth. Season to taste. Thin with creamy milk to the required consistency.

Serve sprinkled with a few freshly chopped herbs and some chive or thyme flowers in season.

### VARIATION

*For a vegetarian version* use vegetable stock, and for a vegan option use extra virgin olive oil instead of the butter and omit the milk.

# LEBANESE COLD CUCUMBER SOUP

Serves 8 to 10

A cooling summer soup that can be adapted to make a little cucumber mousse ring, which in turn can be topped with a variety of good things. Variations of this soup are found all over the Middle East, in Iran, Syria, and Iraq. It's literally made in minutes and can be eaten immediately, but I like to serve it well chilled in small bowls or glasses.

1 large cucumber, organic if possible

¾ cup light cream

¾ cup plain yogurt

1 tablespoon tarragon vinegar (page 74)

1 small garlic clove, crushed

1 tablespoon finely chopped gherkins (optional)

2 tablespoons finely chopped mint

sea salt and freshly ground black pepper

mint sprigs and dried rose petals, to garnish

Using the largest part of a grater, shred the cucumber. Put into a bowl and stir in all the other ingredients save for the mint sprigs and rose petals. Season well. Serve chilled in small glasses, each garnished with a mint sprig and a couple of dried rose petals.

## VARIATION

*Little Cucumber Mousse* Put 2 tablespoons of cold water into a small heat-safe bowl, sprinkle over 2½ teaspoons gelatin powder, and let soak for a few minutes until the water has absorbed the water and feels spongy to the touch. Place the bowl in a small saucepan of simmering water, and when the liquid becomes clear, add a couple of tablespoons of the soup mixture and stir well, then combine the gelatin mixture with the remaining soup. Pour into small glasses—I fill 3½-ounce glasses three-quarters full. Cover and refrigerate until set, 3 to 4 hours. Garnish with a salad of some freshly chopped walnuts and dried rose petals.

# SMOKED TROUT cucumber & horseradish cream salad

A simple but delicious combination, and easy to assemble. The horseradish cream cuts the richness of the trout. It is a mild horseradish sauce, but if you would like something that will really clear the sinuses, just increase the quantity of grated horseradish.

1 to 2 cucumbers

a sprinkle of white wine vinegar

pinch of granulated sugar

1 teaspoon freshly chopped fennel or
   2 teaspoons freshly chopped dill weed,
   plus more to garnish

8 smoked trout fillets

sea salt and freshly ground black pepper

*For the horseradish cream*

1½ to 3 tablespoons peeled and grated horseradish

2 teaspoons white wine vinegar

¼ teaspoon lemon juice

¼ teaspoon mustard

3 teaspoons salt

pinch of freshly ground black pepper

1 teaspoon granulated sugar

1 cup softly whipped cream

*For the garnish*

salmon caviar (optional)

lemon wedges

First make the horseradish cream: In a bowl, combine the grated horseradish with the vinegar, lemon juice, mustard, salt, freshly ground pepper, and sugar. Fold in the softly whipped cream, but do not overmix or the sauce will curdle. The sauce will keep for 2 to 3 days in the refrigerator and may also be served with roast beef. Cover the sauce tightly so that it doesn't pick up flavors in the refrigerator.

Thinly slice the cucumbers (with the peel on). Sprinkle with a few drops of vinegar and season with sugar, salt, and a bit of freshly ground pepper, and stir in the fennel or dill weed.

Assemble the salad: Lay a fillet or a few chunks of smoked trout on each plate. Add some cucumber salad and a spoonful of fresh horseradish cream. Top with salmon caviar, if using. Garnish with lemon wedges and extra fennel or dill weed.

# CRUDITÉS WITH AIOLI

This is one of my favorite appetizers—small helpings of very crisp vegetables with a good garlicky homemade aioli. It fulfills all my criteria for a first course: Plates of crudités look tempting, taste delicious, and, provided the helpings are small, are not too filling. Better still, it's actually good for you, so you can feel very virtuous instead of feeling pangs of guilt!

Another bonus is that I've discovered children love crudités. They even love aioli as long as they don't hear some grown-up saying how much they dislike garlic. You can feel happy to see your children polishing off plates of raw vegetables for supper that are really quick to prepare and bursting with vitamins and minerals.

Crudités can be a perfect appetizer for winter or summer, but to be really delicious you must choose very crisp and fresh organic vegetables. Cut the vegetables into bite-size pieces so they can be picked up easily. There is no need for cutlery because they can be eaten with fingers. The Italian version of crudités is called pinzimonio—just serve them with a bowl of the very best extra virgin olive oil you can find instead of the aioli.

*Use as many of the following as are in season:*
tomatoes quartered, or whole with the calyx on
    if they are freshly picked
purple sprouting broccoli or broccolini,
    broken (not cut) into florets
calabrese (green sprouting broccoli),
    broken into florets
cauliflower, broken into florets
green beans or snow peas
asparagus
baby carrots, or larger carrots peeled and cut into
    2-inch sticks
cucumber, cut into 2-inch sticks
zucchini blossoms
tiny scallions, trimmed
red cabbage, cut into strips
celery stalks, cut into 2-inch sticks
Belgian endive
radicchio
fennel bulb, thinly sliced
red or yellow bell pepper, cored, seeded,
    and cut into 2-inch strips

very fresh Brussels sprouts, cut into halves
    or quarters
whole radishes, with green tops left on
flat-leaf parsley, finely chopped
thyme, finely chopped
chives, finely chopped
watercress sprigs
*For the aioli*
2 large organic, free-range egg yolks (reserve the
    whites for making meringue)
pinch of English mustard powder or ¼ teaspoon
    French mustard
1 to 4 garlic cloves, depending on size, finely
    crushed
¼ teaspoon salt
2 teaspoons white wine vinegar
1 cup sunflower or olive oil
    or a mixture—I use ⅔ cup sunflower oil
    and ⅓ cup extra virgin olive oil
2 teaspoons freshly chopped flat-leaf parsley
freshly ground black pepper

*continued overleaf*

First make the aioli: Put the egg yolks into a Pyrex bowl with the mustard, garlic, salt, and white wine vinegar. Put the oil into a measuring cup with a good pouring spout. Take a wire whisk in one hand and the oil in the other and drip the oil onto the egg yolks, drop by drop, whisking continuously. Within a minute you will notice that the mixture is beginning to thicken. When this happens you can add the oil a bit faster, but don't get too cheeky or it will suddenly split because the egg yolks can only absorb the oil at a certain pace. Taste and add a touch more seasoning and vinegar if necessary.

If the aioli splits it will suddenly become quite thin, and if left sitting the oil will start to float to the top of the sauce. If this happens, you can quite easily rectify the situation by putting another egg yolk or 1 to 2 tablespoons of boiling water into a clean bowl, then whisk in the curdled aioli, ½ teaspoon at a time, until it re-emulsifies. Add the chopped parsley and season to taste.

A typical plate of crudités might include the following: A baby carrot or 4 carrot sticks, 2 Belgian endive or radicchio leaves or fennel bulb slices, 2 cucumber sticks, 1 whole radish with a bit of green leaf left on, 1 tiny tomato or 2 quarters, 1 Brussels sprout cut into quarters, sprouting broccoli or romanesco florets, 1 watercress sprig, and a small pile of chopped fresh herbs.

Wash and prepare the vegetables. Arrange on individual white side plates in contrasting colors, with a spoonful or bowl of aioli in the center.

Alternatively, prepare a large dish or basket for the center of the table. Arrange small mounds of each vegetable in contrasting colors. Place a bowl of aioli in the center and guests can help themselves. Instead of serving the aioli in a bowl, you could make an edible container by cutting a slice off the top of a tomato and hollowing out the seeds. Alternatively, cut a slice of cucumber 1½ inches thick and hollow out the center with a melon baller or a teaspoon. Then fill or pipe the aioli into the tomato or cucumber. Arrange the aioli in the center of the plate of crudités. It's a bit 1950s but delicious nevertheless.

## VARIATION

*Suitable for vegetarians* For a vegan version substitute olive oil for the aioli, as in pinzimonio, a Tuscan appetizer. Fresh, crunchy vegetables are dipped into a bowl of the finest Tuscan extra virgin olive oil—fennel bulb, asparagus, baby carrots, celery stalks... simple but delicious.

# RILLETTES OF FRESH & SMOKED SALMON

Serves 16 to 20

This is a terrific standby recipe that can be tarted up in all sorts of ways or simply slathered on hot thin toast or crusty bread. The texture of this pâté should be coarse and slightly stringy—it should resemble that of pork rillettes, where the meat is torn into shreds with forks rather than blended. Don't be spooked by the amount of butter you use—you're not going to eat it all yourself!

1⅔ cups (3⅓ sticks) salted butter, softened

12 ounces smoked wild or organic salmon

1 tablespoon water

12 ounces freshly cooked wild salmon fillet

a good grating of nutmeg

lemon juice, to taste

freshly chopped fennel (optional)

sea salt and freshly ground black pepper

clarified butter (page 185—optional)

dill weed or fennel fronds and flowers, to garnish

hot, thin sourdough toast, to serve

In a small saucepan, melt 2 tablespoons of the butter. Add the smoked salmon and the water, cover, and cook until it no longer looks opaque, 3 to 4 minutes. Let cool completely.

In a mixing bowl, cream the remaining butter. With two forks, shred the fresh and smoked salmon and combine well. Add to the creamed butter still using a fork (do not use a food processor). Season with salt, freshly ground pepper, and lots of freshly grated nutmeg. Taste and add lemon juice as necessary, and a bit of freshly chopped fennel if you have it.

Serve in individual pots or in a ceramic terrine. Cover with a layer of clarified butter if desired. The rillettes will keep perfectly in the refrigerator for 5 to 6 days provided they are sealed with clarified butter.

Garnish with dill weed or fennel fronds and flowers in season. To serve, toast or chargrill a slice of sourdough bread and spread with the rillettes. Salmon rillettes may be frozen, but use within a few weeks.

## VARIATIONS

*Salmon Rillettes with Cucumber Slices* Cut 2 cucumbers into slices ¼ inch thick. Spoon some of the rillettes onto each cucumber slice. Garnish with chervil sprigs and fennel, dill weed, chive, or wild garlic (ramps) flowers in season. Arrange three slices on a plate with a bit of salad in the center or serve as an appetizer or canapé.

*Extra-Posh Salmon Rillettes* Line 12 to 16 molds 2 inches in diameter, 1 inch deep, with plastic wrap. Place a slice of smoked salmon in each mold. Fill the molds with the rillettes; fold the ends of the smoked salmon over the rillettes to cover. Cover with plastic wrap and refrigerate for at least an hour. Serve with dill pickles.

# MUSHROOM CROSTINI with arugula & Parmesan

Who doesn't love mushrooms on toast? Virtually all fungi are delicious served in this way, so this can be very humble or very exotic depending on the variety chosen. Nowadays I prefer to char the bread on a hot grill pan, then rub with a clove of garlic, but the original version is also delicious.

2 slices sourdough or a large good-quality baguette
extra virgin olive oil
butter, garlic butter, or marjoram butter
   (see method), for sautéing
4 to 6 portobello or large oyster mushrooms
freshly chopped sweet marjoram (optional)

1 garlic clove, crushed (optional), plus 1, halved
arugula leaves
freshly shaved or grated Parmesan cheese,
   Parmigiano Reggiano if possible
sea salt and freshly ground black pepper

Char the sourdough on a hot grill pan. Alternatively, in a skillet, heat 1 inch of olive oil until just below smoking point and fry the bread slices one at a time, removing them just as soon as they become golden. Drain on paper towels and keep warm. (The oil may be strained and used again for another purpose.)

In a skillet, heat a splash of olive oil or olive oil and butter. Remove the stems from the mushrooms and place them skin side down on the pan in a single layer, then add a small dot of butter to each one. Or, better still, use garlic or marjoram butter—simply mix a bit of chopped garlic and parsley or sweet marjoram into some butter. Alternatively, sprinkle with freshly chopped marjoram and a crushed garlic clove. Season with salt and freshly ground pepper.

Cook first on one side (the length of time will depend on the size of the mushroom—3 to 6 minutes), then turn over as soon as you notice that the gills are covered with droplets of juice. Cook on the other side until tender.

Meanwhile, rub the surface of the warm crostini with the garlic clove halves and place on two hot plates. Arrange a few fresh arugula leaves on each one and top with the overlapping mushrooms. Sprinkle on a few more arugula leaves and a bit of freshly shaved or grated Parmesan, and serve right away. If there are any buttery drippings in the pan, spoon every drop over the mushrooms for extra deliciousness.

### VARIATION

*Suitable for vegetarians* if you use a vegetarian alternative to the Parmesan. For a vegan version, omit the butter and cheese.

# SHRIMP ON BROWN BREAD
with homemade mayonnaise

Serves 4

Don't dismiss this very simple appetizer. Spanking fresh shrimp are wonderful served on good brown bread with a homemade mayonnaise. If the shrimp come with roe attached, use some for garnish. Alternatively, serve the freshly cooked shrimp still in their shells with brown bread and homemade mayonnaise.

6 ounces plump shrimp, freshly cooked

4 slices brown bread, thinly sliced, crusts removed
   and spread with butter

4 leaves butterhead, oak leaf, or red leaf lettuce

3 tablespoons Homemade Mayonnaise (page 146)

4 lemon wedges and watercress, flat-leaf parsley,
   fennel, or garden cress sprigs, to garnish

Peel and devein the cooked shrimp. Put a slice of buttered bread on a plate, arrange 1 or 2 lettuce leaves on top, and place 5 or 6 shrimp on the lettuce. Pipe a coil of homemade mayonnaise on the shrimp, just enough so that the proportion of each ingredient looks right. Garnish with lemon wedges and watercress, flat-leaf parsley, fennel, or garden cress sprigs.

### VARIATION

*Shrimp Canapés* Tiny versions of these on circles or squares of bread make a delicious canapé to go with drinks.

# BALLYMALOE CHICKEN LIVER PÂTÉ
with crostini

Serves 10 to 12

My goodness, how this recipe has stood the test of time—it has been our house pâté at Ballymaloe since the opening of the restaurant in 1964! Served in many different ways, its success depends upon being generous with good Irish butter. Sherry can be delicious instead of brandy occasionally. It is essential to cover chicken liver pâté with a layer of clarified or even just melted butter, otherwise the pâté will oxidize and become bitter in taste and gray in color.

8 ounces fresh organic chicken livers
1 large garlic clove, crushed
1 teaspoon thyme leaves
2 tablespoons brandy

1 to 1¼ cups salted butter (depending on how strong the chicken livers are), plus more for cooking
freshly ground black pepper
clarified butter (page 185), to seal the top

Wash the chicken livers in cold water and remove any membrane or green-tinged bits. Dry on paper towels.

In a skillet, melt a pat of butter. When it foams, add the livers and cook over gentle heat. Be careful not to overcook them or the outsides will get crusty; all trace of pink should be gone. Add the crushed garlic and thyme leaves to the pan, stir, and then deglaze the pan with the brandy. Carefully ignite with a long match or reduce for 2 to 3 minutes. Using a spatula, scrape everything into a blender or food processor. Blend for a few seconds, then let cool.

Add 1 cup of butter, cut into cubes, and blend until smooth. Season to taste. This pâté should taste fairly mild and be silky smooth in texture, so add the extra butter if necessary. Serve in small ramekins or glass pots, or in one large terrine. Tap on the work surface to knock out any air bubbles. Spoon some clarified butter over the top of the pâté to seal.

The pâté may also be formed into a roll, wrapped in plastic wrap or wax paper, and refrigerated until firm. When ready to serve, remove the paper and decorate the roll of pâté with finely chopped herbs and herb flowers.

Serve with crostini, toast, or sourdough. This pâté will keep for 4 to 5 days in the refrigerator.

### VARIATION

*Chicken Liver Pâté with Pedro Ximénez Jelly* Soak 1 sheet of gelatin in cold water until soft, 4 to 5 minutes, then strain off the water. In a saucepan, gently warm ⅔ cup Pedro Ximénez sherry, add the gelatin, and let melt. Let cool, then spoon over the top of each ramekin of pâté instead of the butter.

# WARM BACON & AVOCADO SALAD
## with walnut oil dressing

Serves 6

Warm salads were all the rage in the late eighties and early nineties, but they still make a delicious appetizer or light lunch—this simple combination was, and remains, one of my firm favorites. The larger the selection of your salad greens, the more interesting the salad will be.

selection of lettuces and salad greens, such as butterhead, iceberg, Belgian endive, radicchio, trevisano, watercress, and salad burnet

6 ounces slab bacon, unsmoked or lightly smoked

clarified butter (page 185), or a mixture of butter and oil, plus olive oil, for cooking the bacon

4 slices good white bread

sunflower or olive oil, for cooking the croutons

1 large (or 2 small) avocado

18 fresh walnut halves, to garnish (optional)

*For the walnut oil dressing*

3 tablespoons walnut oil or a mixture of 2 tablespoons walnut oil and 1 tablespoon sunflower oil

1 tablespoon Chardonnay wine vinegar

1 teaspoon freshly chopped chives

1 teaspoon freshly chopped flat-leaf parsley

sea salt and freshly ground black pepper

Wash and dry the salad greens, then tear into bite-size pieces. Put into a bowl, cover, and refrigerate until needed.

Cut the rind off the bacon, then cut the bacon into ¼-inch cubes. In a skillet, cook in clarified butter or a mixture of butter and oil until golden. Drain on paper towels.

Make the croutons: Cut the crusts off the bread, then cut into strips ¼ inch wide and into exact cubes. In a skillet, heat at least ¾ inch sunflower or olive oil until almost smoking. Add the croutons to the hot oil and stir once or twice; they will color almost immediately. Place a strainer over a Pyrex or stainless steel bowl. When the croutons are golden brown, pour the oil and croutons into the strainer. Drain the croutons on paper towels. The croutons may be made several hours or even a day ahead.

Make the walnut oil dressing: In a small bowl, beat together the liquid ingredients, then add the chopped herbs and season with salt and freshly ground pepper.

Halve the avocado and remove the pit. Peel and cut into ½-inch dice.

To serve, toss the salad greens in just enough of the dressing to make them glisten. Add the crisp, warm croutons and the diced avocado. Toss gently and divide the salad among six plates. In a hot skillet, recook the bacon in a splash of olive oil until crisp and golden, then scatter the hot bacon over the salad. Garnish with the walnut halves, if desired. Serve right away.

# ONION BHAJIS with tomato & chili relish

Bhajis are street food in India, eaten immediately hot and crisp from the karahi in a newspaper package. Here we serve them as a first course or small plate with a tomato and chili sauce. Cheap, cheerful, and delicious!

¾ cup plus 2 tablespoons all-purpose flour

2 teaspoons baking powder

1 teaspoon chili powder or smoked paprika

2 large organic, free-range eggs, beaten

⅔ cup water

4 onions, peeled and thinly sliced into rings

1 tablespoon freshly snipped chives or cilantro

oil, for deep-frying

sea salt and freshly ground black pepper

*For the tomato & chili relish*

2 medium-size green chilies, seeded and chopped

1 red bell pepper, seeded and cut into ¼-inch dice

½ (14½-ounce) can diced tomatoes

1 garlic clove, crushed

2 teaspoons white sugar

2 teaspoons brown sugar

1 tablespoon white wine vinegar

2 tablespoons water

First make the relish: In a stainless steel saucepan, combine all the relish ingredients, season, and let simmer until reduced by half, about 10 minutes.

Sift the flour, baking powder, and chili powder or smoked paprika into a mixing bowl. Make a hollow in the center and add the eggs. Gradually add the water and beat to make a smooth batter. Stir in the thinly sliced onions and chives or cilantro. Season well with salt and freshly ground pepper.

Just before serving, in a deep fryer or large saucepan, heat the oil to about 340°F. Add dessertspoonfuls of the batter to the hot oil and fry until crisp and golden, about 5 minutes each side. Remove with a slotted spoon and drain on paper towels. Serve hot or cold with the tomato and chili relish.

# LYDIA'S TRADITIONAL IRISH SALAD

Serves 4

This simple old-fashioned salad is the sort of thing you would have had in Ireland for tea on a visit to your Granny on a Sunday evening—perhaps with a slice of meat left over from the Sunday roast. It is still one of my absolute favorites. It's super delicious made with a crisp lettuce, ripe homegrown tomatoes and cucumbers, organic eggs, and homemade canned beets. If, on the other hand, you make it with pale eggs from caged hens, watery tomatoes, tired lettuce and cucumber, and (worst of all) vinegary beet from a jar, you'll wonder why you bothered.

In summer we serve it as an appetizer in Ballymaloe House, with an old-fashioned salad dressing that would have been popular before the days of mayonnaise. It brings back happy nostalgic memories for many people. The salad dressing recipe came from Lydia Strangman, the last occupant of our house.

2 large organic, free-range eggs

1 head butterhead lettuce, leaves separated

2 to 4 ripe sweet tomatoes, quartered

16 cucumber slices

4 radishes, sliced

¼ cup sliced pickled beets and onions

4 tiny scallions

watercress sprigs

freshly chopped flat-leaf parsley

*For Lydia Strangman's salad cream dressing*

2 large organic, free-range eggs

1 tablespoon dark brown sugar

pinch of sea salt

1 teaspoon English mustard powder

1 tablespoon brown malt vinegar

¼ to ½ cup heavy cream

Bring a small saucepan of water to a boil, gently slide in all four eggs, and boil for 7 minutes. Remove two so they are still soft in the center. Boil the other two eggs for another 3 minutes. Strain off the hot water and cover the eggs with cold water. Peel when cold.

Next make the dressing: Cut two of the 10-minute eggs in half and rub the yolks through a strainer into a bowl. Add the sugar, salt, and mustard. Beat in the vinegar and cream. Chop the egg whites and add some to the dressing, reserving the remainder to scatter over the salad. Cover until needed.

Assemble the salads: First arrange a few lettuce leaves on each of four plates. Add a few tomato quarters, half a hard-cooked egg, a few slices of cucumber, and a radish to each plate, plus (preferably just before serving) slices of pickled beet and onion. Garnish with the scallions and watercress sprigs. Scatter with the egg white reserved from the dressing and some chopped parsley. Add a spoon of salad cream dressing to each plate and serve immediately, while the salad is crisp and before the beet starts to run. Serve the extra dressing in a large bowl.

poultry

# TURKEY BAKED WITH MARJORAM

Serves 12 to 14

This casserole roasting technique is a totally brilliant way of cooking not only turkey but also chicken, pheasant, and guinea hen. You'll have lots of flavorful juices as the base for a delicious sauce. This whole dish can be prepped ahead, covered, and reheated. Use the turkey carcass and giblets if you have them. There are several varieties of marjoram; the one we use for this recipe is the annual sweet or knotted marjoram—*Origanum majorana*.

1¼ cups kosher or sea salt (optional)

3¾ quarts water (optional)

1 (10 to 12-pound) organic, free-range turkey, neck and giblets removed

2 to 3 sweet marjoram sprigs

½ cup (1 stick) salted butter, softened

¼ cup freshly chopped marjoram, plus more to garnish

3¾ cups light cream

sea salt and freshly ground black pepper

If you have time, brine the turkey overnight, as it's so worthwhile for the extra depth of flavor. In a very large stainless steel stock pot or plastic bucket, mix the salt with the water until dissolved. Immerse the bird in the brine, cover the pan or bucket, and refrigerate overnight.

The next day, drain the turkey and pat dry with paper towels. Remove the wishbone from the neck end of the turkey for ease of carving. Also remove the fat from the tail end, season the cavity with salt and freshly ground pepper, and stuff with the marjoram sprigs—there is no need for extra salt if the turkey has been brined.

Preheat the oven to 350°F.

Smear the breast and legs of the turkey with 4 tablespoons of the butter. Place the turkey breast side down in a Dutch oven and cook over gentle heat until the skin on the breast turns golden, 6 to 8 minutes. Turn the other way up and smear with half the chopped marjoram mixed with the remaining butter. Season with salt and freshly ground pepper. Cover with wax paper and a tight-fitting lid. Cook for 2 to 2½ hours. Check if the turkey is cooked; the juices should be clear and there should be no trace of pink between the thigh and the breast.

Remove the turkey to a carving dish and let rest while the sauce is being made. Degrease the cooking juices, add the cream, and bring to a boil, then taste and reduce if necessary to strengthen the flavor. Add the remaining chopped marjoram. Add the drippings from the carving dish to the sauce. Season to taste.

Carve the turkey and lightly coat with the sauce. Garnish with freshly chopped marjoram.

# CHICKEN WITH MUSHROOMS & ROSEMARY

Serves 4

Soaking the chicken breasts in milk gives them a meltingly tender and moist texture. I often serve this with orzo, a pasta that looks like grains of rice, but noodles or fettuccine also work well. The flavor of rosemary varies throughout the year, so start by adding half a tablespoon of freshly chopped rosemary to the sauce, taste, and add more if needed.

4 organic, free-range chicken breast halves

milk

1 tablespoon salted butter

1 small rosemary sprig, plus more sprigs
   to garnish

2 tablespoons chopped shallot or scallion

1½ cups sliced white mushrooms

⅔ cup homemade chicken stock

⅔ cup light cream

½ to 1 tablespoon freshly chopped rosemary

Roux (page 76)

sea salt and freshly ground black pepper

*For the orzo (optional)*

1½ teaspoons salt

1 cup dry orzo

1 to 2 tablespoons salted butter or a drizzle of
   extra virgin olive oil

freshly ground black pepper

1 tablespoon freshly chopped flat-leaf parsley

In a dish, just cover the chicken in milk, cover the dish with plastic wrap, and let soak in the refrigerator for about 1 hour. Drain, pat dry with paper towels, and season with salt and pepper.

In a sauté pan, heat most of the butter until foaming, add the chicken, and turn in the butter (but do not brown). Add the rosemary sprig and cover with a circle of wax paper and the lid. Cook over gentle heat until just barely cooked, about 5 to 7 minutes.

Meanwhile, in a skillet, gently sweat the shallot or scallion in the remaining butter. Remove to a plate. Increase the heat, add the mushrooms, season with salt and freshly ground pepper, and cook for 3 to 4 minutes. Add to the shallot or scallion and set aside.

Prepare the orzo: In a large pot, bring 2 to 3 quarts water to a fast rolling boil and add the salt. Sprinkle in the orzo and cook until just tender, 8 to 10 minutes. Drain, rinse under hot water, and toss with the butter or extra virgin olive oil. Season with freshly ground pepper and add the freshly chopped parsley.

When the chicken is cooked, remove to a plate, discarding the rosemary. Add the chicken stock and cream to the saucepan with the chopped rosemary. Bring to a boil and whisk in a small amount of roux—just enough to thicken the sauce slightly. (If the sauce is too thick, add some chicken stock to thin to a light coating consistency.) When you are happy with the flavor and texture of the sauce, return the chicken and mushroom mixture, simmer for 1 to 2 minutes, and season to taste. Serve right away, garnished with rosemary sprigs and with the orzo alongside.

# FARMHOUSE CHICKEN

Serves 8

A whole meal in a dish, this was, and still is, a favorite family supper in our house.
I often serve it in the big black roasting pan on the table, family style.

1 (3½-pound) organic, free-range chicken
1¼ pounds slab bacon
2 tablespoons sunflower oil
seasoned all-purpose flour
14 ounces onions, peeled and finely sliced
   or chopped

¾ pound carrots, peeled and cut into slices
   ½ inch thick
about 5 pounds large floury potatoes, such as
   russet or Idaho
5 cups homemade chicken stock, boiling
sea salt and freshly ground black pepper
1 tablespoon freshly chopped parsley, to garnish

Preheat the oven to 450°F.

Cut the chicken into 8 pieces, then cut the wings apart at the joints so they will cook evenly. Cut the rind off the bacon, then cut 1 pound of the bacon into lardons and the remainder into slices ¼ inch thick. If salty, blanch in a pot of boiling water, drain, and refresh in cold water. Dry on paper towels. Set the slices aside.

In a wide skillet, heat the oil and cook the lardons until the fat begins to run and they are pale golden. Transfer to a plate. Toss the chicken pieces in the seasoned flour and sauté in the bacon fat and oil until golden on both sides. Remove from the pan and put with the bacon. Finally, toss the onions and carrots in the bacon fat for 1 to 2 minutes.

Peel the potatoes and cut just under half of them into slices ¼ inch thick. Arrange a layer of potato slices on the bottom of a deep roasting pan. Season with salt and freshly ground pepper. Top with a layer of the seasoned chicken pieces. Cut the remaining potatoes lengthwise into slices 1½ inches thick and arrange cut side up on top of the chicken (the whole top of the dish should be covered with potato slices). Season with salt and freshly ground pepper. Pour the boiling chicken stock into the roasting pan.

Bake for about 1 hour. After 30 minutes of cooking, top with the bacon slices so they get deliciously crisp with the potatoes. Test for doneness after 1 hour—it may take a little longer. Cover the pan loosely with parchment paper near the end of cooking if the top is getting too brown. The vegetables will have absorbed much of the stock, but the dish should still be moist and juicy underneath the crisp potatoes and bacon slices on top. Sprinkle with the chopped parsley and serve.

# CASSEROLE ROAST PHEASANT
with apple & Calvados

Serves 4

This recipe comes from Vallée d'Auge in Normandy in France where they have wonderful rich cream and delicious apples. Chicken or guinea hen may also be used in this recipe. Here, I'm using the brilliant casserole roasting technique again (see page 48).

1 plump young, well-hung pheasant

3 tablespoons salted butter

3½ tablespoons Calvados

1 cup heavy whipping cream or ½ cup cream and
   ½ cup homemade chicken stock

Roux (optional—page 76)

2 apples, such as Golden Delicious or
   Braeburn, peeled, cored, and cut into
   ⅓-inch dice

sea salt and freshly ground black pepper

watercress or chervil sprigs, to garnish

Preheat the oven to 350°F.

Choose a flameproof casserole dish, preferably oval, just large enough to fit the pheasant. Season the cavity, spread 1 tablespoon of the butter over the breast and legs of the pheasant, and place breast side down in the pot. Let it brown over gentle heat, turn over, and sprinkle with salt and freshly ground pepper. Cover with a tight-fitting lid and cook in the oven for 40 to 45 minutes. Check to see that the pheasant is cooked—there should be no trace of pink between the leg and the breast. Transfer the pheasant to a serving dish and keep warm.

Carefully strain and degrease the drippings in the pot. Bring to a boil, add the Calvados, and carefully ignite with a long match. Shake the pan and when the flames have subsided add the cream or cream and stock. Reduce until the sauce thickens to a light coating consistency, stirring occasionally; taste for seasoning. The sauce may also be thickened by whisking in a bit of roux.

In a skillet, cook the apple in the remaining butter over medium heat until golden.

Carve the pheasant and arrange on a hot serving dish or individual plates. Coat with the sauce. Place the apple in the center and garnish the dish with watercress or chervil sprigs.

# POACHED TURKEY WITH MUSHROOMS

Serves 20 to 25

Another gem, this is a brilliant and delicious party dish. Make it ahead and reheat for stress-free entertaining.

1 (10-pound) organic, free-range turkey

3½ quarts homemade light chicken stock or water

2 large carrots, peeled and sliced

2 large onions, peeled and quartered

2 celery stalks

1 bouquet garni made up of 6 parsley stems,
   2 thyme sprigs, 1 small bay leaf, and
   1 tarragon sprig

10 black peppercorns

2 pounds mushrooms

2½ to 4 tablespoons salted butter

3¾ cups light cream or creamy milk

½ cup Roux (optional—page 76)

sea salt and freshly ground black pepper

flat-leaf parsley, chervil, or watercress sprigs,
   to garnish

Put the turkey into a Dutch oven. Pour in the chicken stock or water and add the carrots, onions, celery, bouquet garni, and peppercorns. Season with salt and freshly ground pepper. Bring to a boil, cover, and simmer on the stovetop or cook in a preheated oven at 350°F for 2 to 2½ hours.

When the turkey is cooked, remove from the pot and then strain and degrease the cooking liquid. Discard the vegetables—they will have given their flavor to the broth already. Return the liquid to the pot and reduce by half.

Meanwhile, slice the mushrooms. In a very hot skillet, sauté the mushrooms in the butter, then set aside.

Add the cream or creamy milk to the turkey poaching liquid and reduce again, uncovered, for 5 to 10 minutes. Stir in the sautéed mushrooms.

Skin the turkey, carve the flesh into 2-inch pieces, and add to the sauce. Return to a boil and season to taste. (The boiling sauce can be thickened to the required consistency by whisking in the roux, rather than by reducing, if desired.) Transfer to a hot serving dish and garnish with parsley, chervil, or watercress. Serve with a good green salad, rice pilaf, or potatoes.

Alternatively, divide the turkey among several large serving dishes; if mashed potato is spooned around the edges, it's a whole meal in one dish. Refrigerate until ready to serve, then reheat in a preheated oven at 350°F for 20 to 30 minutes.

# ROAST DUCK with applesauce & red cabbage

Serves 4

This is such a time-honored combination—the slightly tart applesauce cuts the richness of the duck and the braised red cabbage complements the flavor not just of duck but also roast goose and pork with crackling (page 78).

Red cabbage is traditionally in season in the fall and throughout the winter, but is now available year round. Serve with venison, duck, goose, or pork—the flavor is too strong to accompany fish and delicate meats. The recipe for Braised Red Cabbage serves 8 to 10, but it keeps brilliantly. Store in the refrigerator or freeze.

⅓ cup plus 1 tablespoon kosher or sea salt

5 cups water

1 (4-pound) free-range duck

*For the stock*

neck and giblets from the duck

1 onion, peeled and quartered

1 carrot, peeled and sliced

1 bouquet garni made up of parsley stems,
   1 small celery stalk, and 1 thyme sprig

2 to 3 black peppercorns

sea salt and freshly ground black pepper

*For the sage & onion stuffing*

3 tablespoons salted butter

3 ounces onion, peeled and finely chopped

2 cups fresh white bread crumbs

1 tablespoon freshly chopped sage

sea salt and freshly ground black pepper

*For the braised red cabbage*

8 ounces red cabbage

½ tablespoon white wine vinegar

¼ cup water

½ teaspoon salt

1 heaping tablespoon granulated sugar, or more
   to taste

8 ounces baking apples

*For the applesauce*

1 pound baking apples

2 to 4 teaspoons water

about ¼ cup granulated sugar, depending on the
   tartness of the apples

The day before cooking, brine the duck (this will enhance the flavor considerably): In a large stainless steel pan or plastic container, mix the salt with the water until dissolved. Immerse the bird in the brine, cover the pan or container, and let stand in the refrigerator overnight.

You'll need some stock to make a flavorsome gravy, so use the giblets. Put the neck, gizzard, heart, and any other scraps from the duck into a saucepan with the onion, carrot, and bouquet garni. Cover with cold water and add the peppercorns but no salt. Bring slowly to a boil, then simmer for 2 to 3 hours. This will make a delicious stock that will be the basis of the gravy.

*continued overleaf*

Meanwhile, drain the duck and pat dry with paper towels. Using tweezers, remove any remaining feathers if necessary. Preheat the oven to 350°F.

Make the stuffing: In a saucepan, melt the butter, add the onion, and sweat over gentle heat until soft but not colored, 5 to 10 minutes. Add the bread crumbs and sage. Season with salt and freshly ground pepper to taste. Unless you plan to cook the duck immediately, let the stuffing cool completely.

Season the cavity of the duck with salt and freshly ground pepper and spoon in the stuffing. Truss the duck loosely. Place in a roasting pan and roast in the oven for about 1½ hours.

Make the braised red cabbage: Discard any damaged outer leaves from the cabbage. Wash the cabbage if necessary. Cut into quarters, remove the core, and finely slice across the grain. In a cast-iron casserole dish or stainless steel saucepan, combine the vinegar, water, salt, and sugar. Add the cabbage and bring to a boil.

Meanwhile, peel and core the apples, then cut into quarters (no smaller). Lay them on top of the cabbage, cover, and continue to cook gently until the cabbage is tender, 30 to 50 minutes. Do not overcook or the color and flavor will be ruined. Season to taste and add more sugar if necessary.

Make the applesauce: Peel, quarter, and core the apples. Cut the pieces in half and put into a small stainless steel or cast-iron saucepan with the water and sugar. Cover and cook over low heat. As soon as the apple has broken down, beat into a puree, stir, and taste for sweetness.

When the duck is cooked, transfer to a serving dish and let rest while you make the gravy. Degrease the drippings (keep the precious duck fat for roast or sautéed potatoes). Add the stock to the drippings in the roasting pan and bring to a boil. Taste and season if necessary. Strain the gravy into a sauceboat and serve right away with the duck, alongside the braised red cabbage and applesauce.

# CASSEROLE ROAST CHICKEN with leeks & bacon

Serves 4 to 6

Another delicious casserole roast chicken recipe. Replace the bacon with chorizo or merguez sausage for a more gutsy flavor.

1 pound leeks, trimmed

8 ounces bacon

1 (3¼-pound) organic, free-range chicken

1 tablespoon salted butter

a splash of sunflower oil

1 cup homemade chicken stock or water

1 cup light cream

Roux (page 76)

sea salt and freshly ground black pepper

¼ cup freshly chopped flat-leaf parsley, to garnish

Preheat the oven to 350°F.

Slice the white parts of the leeks into rounds and wash them well. Cut the rind from the bacon, then cut the bacon into ½-inch cubes.

Remove the fat from inside the tail end of the chicken and discard. Season with salt and freshly ground pepper. Rub the butter over the breast and legs of the chicken and place it breast side down in a Dutch oven. Brown over gentle heat; this can take 5 to 6 minutes. As soon as the breast is golden, remove the chicken from the pot and set aside. Add the pieces of bacon to the pot with the oil. Cook the bacon until the fat runs and the bacon is golden, then add the sliced leeks and toss together in the bacon fat. Season with freshly ground pepper, but no salt as the bacon will probably be salty enough. Then replace the chicken on top of the leeks and bacon. Cover the pot and roast in the oven for 1¼ to 1½ hours.

When the chicken is cooked, remove to a serving dish. Using a slotted spoon, lift out the leeks and bacon and place in the center of a hot serving dish.

Skim the drippings of all fat, add the stock or water and cream, and bring to a boil. Thicken by whisking in a small amount of roux. The sauce should not be too thick, just thick enough to lightly coat the back of a spoon. Let simmer over low heat while you carve the chicken.

Carve the chicken into 4 to 6 servings, depending on how hungry you all are; everyone should get a portion of white and brown meat. Arrange the leeks and bacon around the chicken. Taste the sauce and add a bit more salt and freshly ground pepper if necessary. If the sauce has become too thick, add some water. Spoon the hot sauce over the chicken, sprinkle with the chopped parsley, and serve.

# CHICKEN WITH ROSEMARY & TOMATOES

Serves 4 to 6

*I love this chicken dish. Increase the quantity of potatoes and onions to make a more substantial dish, or try using pheasant or guinea hen for a more gamey flavor.*

1 (3½-pound) organic, free-range chicken

2 tablespoons salted butter

3 onions

3 potatoes

5 to 6 very ripe tomatoes

1 tablespoon extra virgin olive oil

1 rosemary sprig, finely chopped, or 1 teaspoon thyme leaves

sea salt and freshly ground black pepper

flat-leaf parsley or sweet marjoram sprigs, to garnish

Preheat the oven to 350°F.

If possible, remove the wishbone from the neck end of the chicken for ease of carving. Remove the fat from the tail end of the chicken and set aside. Season the cavity with salt and freshly ground pepper. Smear the breast with half the butter, place the chicken breast side down in a Dutch oven (preferably an oval one that will just fit the chicken), and brown over gentle heat for 5 to 6 minutes.

Meanwhile, peel the onions and potatoes, then thickly slice along with the tomatoes. Remove the chicken to a plate and add the remaining butter and the extra virgin olive oil to the pot. Toss the potatoes, onions, and tomatoes in the fat and oil. Sprinkle with the chopped rosemary or thyme leaves, salt, and freshly ground pepper. Cover and cook for 5 to 6 minutes. Place the chicken on top of the vegetables and cover. Cook in the oven for about 1¼ hours.

Carve the chicken and serve with the potatoes, tomatoes, and onions. Degrease the drippings, bring to a boil, and spoon over the chicken and vegetables. Serve sprinkled with flat-leaf parsley or marjoram sprigs.

Good to know: The organic chicken fat can be rendered down in a low oven (275°F) and used to roast or sauté potatoes.

# CHICKEN PILAF

Serves 8

A brilliant recipe but you'll need a really flavorful chicken for this—we often use our "old hens," two-year-old fowl that have come to the end of their egg-laying life and have a deep, rich flavor; the type of bird that the French love to use for coq au vin. Because of their age they need to be poached rather than roasted, otherwise the meat can be tough.

This dish is great for a party. Although a risotto can be made in 20 minutes, it entails 20 minutes of pretty continuous stirring, which makes it feel rather labor-intensive. A pilaf on the other hand looks after itself once the initial cooking is underway. The pilaf is versatile—serve it as a staple or add whatever tasty bits you have on hand. Beware of using pilaf as a garbage can; all additions should be carefully seasoned and balanced. It may be prepared ahead and reheats well, but do not add the liaison until just before serving.

⅓ cup plus 1 tablespoon kosher or sea salt
   (optional)
5 cups water (optional)
1 (4 to 4¼-pound) organic stewing hen or organic,
   free-range chicken
1 large carrot, peeled and sliced
1 large onion, peeled and sliced
5 black peppercorns
1 bouquet garni made up of 1 thyme sprig,
   parsley stems, 1 tiny bay leaf, and 1 celery stalk
2 to 2½ cups water, or a mixture of water and white
   wine, or homemade light chicken stock
1 to 1¼ cups light cream or creamy milk
2 tablespoons Roux (page 76)
sea salt and freshly ground black pepper
watercress sprigs, to serve

*For the rice pilaf*
2 tablespoons salted butter
2 tablespoons finely chopped onion or shallot
2¼ cups white long-grain rice (preferably basmati)
1 quart homemade chicken stock
2 tablespoons freshly chopped herbs,
   such as parsley, thyme, or chives (optional)
*For the liaison*
1 large organic, free-range egg yolk
3½ tablespoons heavy whipping cream

If you have time, use the salt and water to brine the chicken overnight, following the directions on page 56. Otherwise, before cooking, season the chicken with salt and freshly ground pepper. Place in a Dutch oven with the carrot, onion, peppercorns, and bouquet garni. Pour in the water, water and wine, or stock (¾ stock to ¼ wine). Cover and bring to a boil, then simmer either on the stovetop or cook in a preheated oven at 350°F for 1½ to 3 hours, depending on the age of the bird. When the bird is cooked, remove from the pot. The meat should be almost falling off the bones.

*continued overleaf*

Meanwhile, make the rice pilaf: In a flameproof casserole dish, melt the butter, add the onion or shallot, and sweat for 2 to 3 minutes. Add the rice and toss for a minute or two, just long enough for the grains to change color. Season with salt and freshly ground pepper, add the chicken stock, cover, and bring to a boil. Reduce the heat to minimum and then simmer on the stovetop or cook in a preheated oven at 325°F for about 10 minutes. By then the rice should be just cooked and all the water absorbed. Just before serving, stir in the fresh herbs if using.

Strain and degrease the chicken cooking liquid, then return to the pot. Discard the vegetables, as they have already given their flavor to the broth. Reduce the liquid until the flavor is concentrated, 5 to 10 minutes. Add the cream or creamy milk, return to a boil, and reduce again. Thicken to a light coating consistency by whisking in the roux. Season to taste with salt.

Skin the chicken and carve the flesh into bite-size pieces; add to the sauce and heat through and bubble (the dish may be prepared ahead to this point).

Finally, just before serving, in a bowl, beat together the egg yolk and cream to make a liaison. Add some of the hot sauce, then carefully stir the liaison into the chicken mixture. Season to taste. Stir well and do not let the sauce boil or it will curdle. Serve with the rice pilaf and watercress sprigs.

# CHICKEN WITH CREAM & LEMON

Serves 4

You'll love this simple recipe that can be made ahead and gently reheated later. The dish can be embellished with asparagus or sea kale in season, or with exotic mushrooms that are available year round. Some chopped sweet marjoram is also wonderful added to the sauce, as is finely chopped watercress. If all cream seems too rich for your palate, use half cream and half rich chicken stock instead.

4 organic, free-range skinless chicken breast halves

2 tablespoons salted butter

1 cup heavy whipping cream

finely grated zest and juice of 1 organic lemon

Roux (optional—page 76)

sea salt and freshly ground black pepper

finely chopped chives and chive blossoms in season, to garnish

Heat a sauté pan just large enough to fit the chicken. Smear the chicken on the skin side with the butter. When the pan is moderately hot, add the chicken to the pan, buttered side down. Cook until pale golden brown. Turn and seal on the other side. Season with salt and freshly ground pepper, cover the pan tightly, and cook over gentle heat until the chicken is just cooked through, 6 to 8 minutes depending on size. Remove the chicken and keep warm.

Add the cream and lemon zest and juice to the pan. Let it bubble up and then simmer until the sauce is slightly thickened. Alternatively, add a bit of roux, just enough to thicken the sauce to a light coating consistency. Season to taste. Slide the warm cooked chicken back into the pan and turn in the sauce, then bubble gently for a minute or two.

Serve immediately with a sprinkling of chopped chives and chive blossoms when available. Alternatively, let cool and refrigerate, then reheat gently when ready to serve. Serve with rice, fresh noodles, or fettuccine.

meat

# GREEK LAMB with onion & lima bean stew

Serves 6

An easy comforting stew that can be adapted and added to—try goat meat if you can source it, which makes a delicious substitute for lamb. I sometimes add a can of tomatoes and their juice, then reduce the stock to ⅔ cup. Add a good pinch of sugar and of course chop the tomatoes. Stir in a heaping tablespoon of sweet marjoram or oregano just before serving.

1¼ cups dry lima beans

2 tablespoons extra virgin olive oil

2½ pounds boneless lamb shoulder, cut into
    1½-inch cubes

1½ pounds pearl onions, peeled

6 whole garlic cloves, peeled

2 bay leaves

1 large thyme sprig

1¾ to 2⅓ cups homemade lamb or chicken
    stock

1 teaspoon sea salt

freshly ground black pepper

coarsely chopped flat-leaf parsley, to garnish

The day before you want to serve the stew, in a bowl, cover the dry beans with plenty of cold water and let soak overnight.

The next day, drain the beans, put into a saucepan, and cover with fresh water. Boil for 10 to 15 minutes while you prepare the meat.

In a sauté pan, heat the olive oil, toss the lamb, onions, and garlic in the hot oil in batches, and transfer to a Dutch oven or large, heavy-bottom pot. Drain the beans and add to the pot with the bay leaves and thyme sprig. Pour in the stock, which should come about halfway up the meat. Add the salt and bring to a boil, then simmer for about 1 hour or until all the ingredients are tender. Season to taste—it may need more seasoning. The stew should be nice and juicy, but if there is more juice than is necessary, remove the lid toward the end of cooking. If the liquid tastes a bit weak, strain it off and reduce to the required strength and quantity in a wide, uncovered pot. Return the meat and beans to the stock, reheat, and season to taste. Sprinkle with the coarsely chopped parsley and serve.

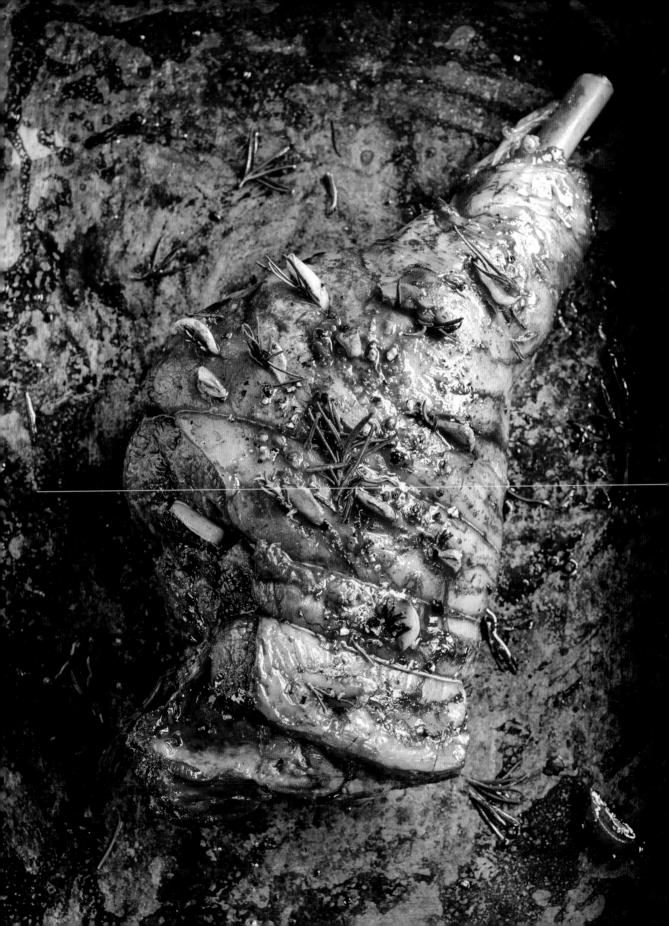

# LAMB ROAST with rosemary & garlic

Serves 8 to 10

Rosemary survives year round even in colder backyards. Spike your leg of lamb with little tufts of this pungent herb and tiny slivers of garlic—delicious hot, warm, or at room temperature. A Ballymaloe classic. A small piece of anchovy wrapped around the rosemary and garlic adds extra flavor.

1 (6 to 7-pound) bone-in whole leg of lamb
3 rosemary sprigs, depending on size
3 to 4 garlic cloves
flaky sea salt and freshly ground black pepper

*For the gravy*
2½ cups homemade lamb stock
Roux (optional—page 76)
sea salt and freshly ground black pepper

Choose a good leg of lamb with a thin layer of fat. Ask the butcher to trim the shank and remove the aitch bone for ease of carving later. With the point of a sharp knife or metal skewer, make deep holes all over the lamb, about 1 inch apart. It is a good idea not to do this on the underside of the roast, in case somebody insists on eating their lamb unflavored. Divide the rosemary sprigs into tufts of three or four leaves together.

Peel the garlic cloves and cut them into small spikes about the same size as a match broken into three. Insert a spike of garlic into each hole with a tuft of rosemary. If you have time, cover and refrigerate for 1 to 2 hours.

Preheat the oven to 350°F. Sprinkle the lamb with flaky sea salt and freshly ground pepper and sit it in a roasting pan. Roast for about 1¼ hours for rosy lamb, or 1½ to 1¾ hours if you want it more well done, depending on the size of the roast. If you own a meat thermometer, it will eliminate guesswork altogether, but ensure the thermometer is not touching a bone when you are testing the internal temperature. For rare lamb it should be 140°F, medium 158°F, and well done 167°F.

Remove the lamb to a serving dish and let rest while you make the gravy.

Spoon the fat off the drippings in the roasting pan. Pour the stock into the pan and boil for a few minutes, stirring and scraping the pan well to dissolve the caramelized drippings (I find a small wire whisk is best for this). Thicken with a very small amount of roux if desired. Season to taste. Strain and serve the gravy separately in a gravy boat. Serve the lamb along with roast potatoes or navy beans.

# STEAK WITH BÉARNAISE SAUCE & frites

Serves 6 to 12, depending on how it's served

This is still *the* classic combination. Of all the sauces to serve with steak, béarnaise is my absolute favorite. The consistency should be considerably thicker than that of hollandaise or beurre blanc, both of which ought to be a light coating consistency. Leftover béarnaise sauce solidifies somewhat, which we refer to as béarnaise butter. Serve a dollop on top of steaks or with roast beef. I find a heavy ridged cast-iron grill pan the best for cooking steaks when you don't need to make a sauce in the pan. Rather than serving a steak whole, I now prefer to slice it thinly and serve the juicy slices over a bed of arugula or watercress with the frites and a few flakes of sea salt sprinkled on top.

6 (6-ounce) New York strip or filet mignon steaks

1 garlic clove

sprinkle of extra virgin olive oil

2¼ pounds potatoes, such as russet or Idaho, peeled and cut into ¼-inch sticks

good-quality sunflower or olive oil, for deep-frying

flaky sea salt and freshly ground black pepper

watercress or arugula leaves (optional), to serve

*For the béarnaise sauce*

¼ cup tarragon vinegar (page 74)

¼ cup dry white wine

2 teaspoons finely chopped shallot

pinch of freshly ground black pepper

2 large organic, free-range egg yolks

½ to ¾ cup (1 to 1½ sticks) salted butter, diced

1 tablespoon freshly chopped French tarragon leaves, plus more to garnish

Prepare the steaks about 1 hour before cooking. Score the fat at 1-inch intervals. Peel the garlic clove, cut in half, and rub both sides of each steak with the garlic. Grind lots of black pepper over the steaks and sprinkle on a few drops of olive oil. Turn the steaks in the oil and set aside at room temperature.

Make the béarnaise sauce: In a shallow, heavy-bottom stainless steel saucepan, boil the vinegar, wine, shallot, and pepper until completely reduced and the pan is almost dry but not brown. Immediately add 1 tablespoon of cold water. Remove the pan from the heat and let cool for 1 to 2 minutes.

Beat in the egg yolks and then add the butter a piece at a time over very low heat, whisking continuously. As soon as one piece melts, add the next piece; the sauce will gradually thicken. If it shows signs of becoming too thick or slightly scrambling, immediately remove from the heat and add a splash of cold water. Do not leave the pan or stop whisking until the sauce is made. Finally, add the tarragon and season to taste. If the sauce is slow to thicken, it may be because you are being too cautious and the heat is too low. Increase the heat slightly and continue to whisk until all the butter is added and the sauce is a thick coating consistency. It is important to

*continued overleaf*

remember, however, that if you are making béarnaise sauce in a saucepan directly over the heat, it should be possible to put your hand on the side of the pan at any stage. If the pan feels too hot for your hand, it's too hot for the sauce.

Another good tip if you are making béarnaise sauce for the first time is to keep a bowl of cold water close by so that you can plunge the bottom of the pan into it if it becomes too hot. Keep the sauce warm in a Pyrex bowl over hot but not simmering water or in a Thermos until you want to serve it.

Heat the grill pan, season the steaks with a little flaky sea salt, and put them onto the hot pan. The approximate cooking times for each side of the strips steaks are: rare—2 minutes; medium rare—3 minutes; medium—4 minutes; and well done—5 minutes. For filet mignon steaks: rare—5 minutes; medium rare—6 minutes; medium—7 minutes; and well done— 8 to 9 minutes. I like to start a strip steak on the fat side and cook until the fat renders out and becomes deliciously crisp, 4 to 5 minutes, then cook on each side to your taste.

Transfer the steak to a plate. Let rest for a few minutes in a warm place while you cook the frites.

In a deep fryer or large saucepan, heat the oil for deep-frying to about 320°F. Deep-fry the potatoes until they are almost soft. Drain, increase the oil temperature to 350 to 375°F, and cook until crisp and golden, another 1 to 2 minutes. Drain on paper towels. Sprinkle lightly with salt.

Serve on hot plates with the béarnaise sauce over the steak or in a small bowl on the side and sprinkle over some chopped tarragon. Serve with the frites and watercress. Alternatively, thinly slice the steak, place on a bed of watercress or arugula leaves, drizzle with béarnaise sauce, and serve as soon as possible.

## TIP

Tarragon vinegar is essential for béarnaise sauce. It's not easy to find but it's super easy to make: Simply push 3 to 4 fresh tarragon sprigs into a bottle of good-quality white wine vinegar and let infuse for 6 to 7 days before using. Some of the pickled tarragon may also be added to the béarnaise sauce. If you do not have tarragon vinegar to hand, use a white wine vinegar and add some more chopped tarragon to the béarnaise sauce.

# HAM STEAK with fried banana & Irish whiskey sauce

Serves 5 to 6

At Ballymaloe House we cure our own free-range saddleback pigs, or we ask our local butcher Frank Murphy to cure it for us, and serve cured loin chops ("bacon chops") with Irish whiskey sauce, but they are also delicious served just with simple fried bananas—it sounds passé, but believe me it's so good. We particularly love to serve them with peperonata and champ. Look for premium aged country ham to use here instead.

1 (2¼-pound) uncooked boneless smoked country
    ham slice, soaked in cold water overnight
1 cup seasoned all-purpose flour
1 large organic, free-range egg, beaten with a
    splash of milk
fresh white bread crumbs or panko crumbs
2 tablespoons clarified butter (page 185) or
    1 tablespoon salted butter and
    1 to 2 tablespoons olive oil, for cooking

*For the fried banana*
1 tablespoon salted butter
2 bananas
*For the Irish whiskey sauce*
1 cup plus 2 tablespoons granulated sugar
5 tablespoons cold water
¼ cup hot water
3 to 4 tablespoons Irish whiskey

Drain the ham slice. In a saucepan, cover the ham slice with fresh cold water and bring to a boil. If the ham is still excessively salty, there will be a white froth on top of the water, so discard the water and start again. After the blanching process, bring the water to a boil and continue to boil until fully cooked, 45 minutes to 1 hour. Remove the rind but not the fat unless there is too much. Slice into steaks ¾ inch thick.

Dip each ham steak in the seasoned flour, then in the beaten egg, and finally coat with bread crumbs. In a heavy skillet, heat the clarified butter or butter and oil and gently cook the ham steaks until they are heated through and golden on both sides, about 4 minutes each side.

Make the fried bananas: In a skillet, melt the butter. Peel the bananas, then split in half lengthwise or cut into thick slices on the bias. Cook gently in the melted butter until soft and slightly golden.

Make the Irish whiskey sauce: In a saucepan, combine the sugar and cold water and stir over gentle heat until the sugar dissolves and the syrup comes to a boil. Remove the spoon and do not stir. Continue to boil until the syrup turns a nice chestnut-brown color. Remove the pan from the heat and immediately add the hot water. Let dissolve again and then add the Irish whiskey. Serve hot or cold alongside the ham steaks and fried banana.

# BALLYMALOE IRISH STEW

Serves 4 to 6

Another classic one-pot dish. The recipe varies from region to region—in Cork, carrots are a quintessential addition, not so in parts of Ulster. Pearl barley is another favorite option, originally added to bulk up the stew. You'll need to add extra stock (1¼ to 2½ cups) if you include it, as it guzzles liquid, but it becomes deliciously plump and flavorful.

3 pounds center-cut lamb leg steaks, no less than 1 inch thick

8 medium or 12 pearl onions, peeled

12 baby carrots, peeled and cut into large chunks

1 to 2 tablespoons dry pearl barley (optional)

3½ to 4¼ cups homemade lamb stock (page 81) or water

8 to 12 large potatoes, or more if desired, peeled

1 thyme sprig

1 tablespoon Roux (see below—optional)

1 tablespoon freshly chopped parsley

1 tablespoon freshly chopped chives

sea salt and freshly ground black pepper

*For the roux*

½ cup (1 stick) salted butter

¾ cup plus 2 tablespoons all-purpose flour, or ⅓ cup cornstarch and ⅓ cup rice flour for a gluten-free roux

Preheat the oven to 350°F, if you plan to finish cooking the stew in the oven.

Cut the lamb steaks in half and trim off some of the excess fat. Set aside. In a heavy skillet, render the lamb fat over gentle heat (discard the rendered-down pieces).

Toss the meat in the hot fat in the pan until it is slightly brown, then transfer to a Dutch oven. Quickly toss the onions and carrots in the fat, and the pearl barley if using. Build up the meat, carrots, and onions (plus pearl barley if using) in layers in the pot, carefully seasoning *each layer* with freshly ground pepper and salt. Deglaze the skillet with the lamb stock or water, bring to a boil, and pour into the pot. Lay the potatoes on top of the stew (they will steam while the stew cooks). Season the potatoes, add the thyme, and bring to a boil on the stovetop. Cover with a wax paper lid and the pot lid. Transfer to the oven or let simmer on the stovetop until the lamb is tender, about 1½ hours.

Make the roux: In a saucepan, melt the butter and cook the all-purpose flour or cornstarch and rice flour in it for 2 minutes over low heat, stirring occasionally. Roux can be stored and used as required or it can be prepared on the spot. It will keep for at least 2 weeks in the refrigerator.

When the stew is cooked, pour off the cooking liquid, degrease, and reheat in another saucepan. Thicken slightly by whisking in the tablespoon of roux. Check the seasoning, then add half the freshly chopped parsley and chives. Pour over the meat and vegetables. Bring the stew back up to a boil and serve from the pot or in a large ceramic dish sprinkled with the remaining chopped herbs. Serve in deep plates with lots of good Irish butter.

# CRACKLING ROAST PORK
with garlic & thyme leaves & applesauce

Serves 10 to 12

Pork belly is less expensive than loin and makes the sweetest and juiciest roast pork. Make sure to buy it with the skin on, otherwise you'll miss out on the cracklings. The trick with applesauce is to cook it covered over low heat with very little water. Applesauce freezes perfectly, so make more than you need and freeze in tiny, plastic cartons. It is also a good way to use up windfalls.

1 (5-pound) boneless whole organic pork belly, preferably heritage

mix or blend of the following: 3 finely chopped garlic cloves, ¼ cup freshly chopped parsley, 1 tablespoon olive oil (add more if needed to make a thick paste), 2 tablespoons thyme leaves, 1 teaspoon flaky sea salt, 1 teaspoon freshly ground black pepper

warm Applesauce (page 56), to serve

*For the gravy*
4¼ cups homemade chicken or pork stock
Roux (optional—page 76)
plenty of freshly chopped herbs, such as parsley and thyme, plus a small quantity of sage

Score the pork skin at ¼-inch intervals—a Stanley knife works brilliantly, otherwise you may want to ask your butcher to do this because the skin of free-range pork can be quite tough. (Scoring will make it easier to carve later.) Rub the herb paste well into the cuts; it should not be sitting on top.

Preheat the oven to 350°F. Roast the pork on a rack over a roasting pan, 28 to 30 minutes per pound. Just before the end of cooking, transfer the pork to another roasting pan and increase the temperature to 450°F to crisp the cracklings.

Make the gravy: Degrease the drippings in the roasting pan and add the stock to deglaze. Bring to a boil, season, and whisk to dissolve any caramelized drippings. Thicken with a bit of roux if desired. Add the freshly chopped herbs to the gravy.

Serve the pork with roast potatoes, preferably cooked in pork lard, and the warm applesauce.

# DINGLE PIE

Serves 6

Mutton and lamb pies were, and still are, traditional in many parts of Co. Kerry, including Dingle and Listowel. Cumin was not part of the original recipe but was an addition by Myrtle Allen, which Ballymaloe House guests loved. The original pie crust was made with lamb suet, but Myrtle substituted butter with delicious results. This pie freezes perfectly for 2 to 3 months, but use sooner rather than later. The quantity of cumin seeds will depend on how fresh the spice is.

1 pound boned lamb or mutton from the
    shoulder or leg, bones reserved for the stock
9 ounces onions
9 ounces carrots
1 to 2 heaping teaspoons cumin seeds
2 tablespoons all-purpose flour
1¼ cups homemade lamb or mutton stock
    (see right)
sea salt and freshly ground black pepper

*For the lamb or mutton stock*
lamb bones from the meat
1 carrot, peeled
1 onion, peeled
outer celery stalk
1 bouquet garni made up of 1 thyme sprig,
    parsley stems, and 1 small bay leaf
*For the hot water pie crust*
2¾ cups all-purpose flour
pinch of salt
¾ cup (1½ sticks) butter, diced
⅓ cup plus 2 tablespoons water
beaten organic, free-range egg, to glaze

First make the stock: In a stock pot, combine the lamb bones, carrot, onion, celery, and bouquet garni. Cover with cold water and let simmer for 3 to 4 hours.

Trim all the surplus fat from the meat and reserve, then dice the meat into small, neat pieces about the size of a small sugar cube. In a hot, wide saucepan, render down the scraps of fat until the fat runs. Discard the remaining solid fat pieces. Peel the onions and carrots, then cut into slightly smaller dice than the meat and toss in the fat. Let cook for 3 to 4 minutes. Remove the vegetables and toss the meat in the remaining fat over high heat until its color changes.

In a hot skillet, dry-roast the cumin for a few minutes. Using a pestle and mortar, crush the seeds lightly. Stir the flour and crushed cumin seeds into the meat and cook gently for 2 minutes. Blend in the stock gradually and bring to a boil, stirring occasionally. Return the vegetables to the pan, season with salt and freshly ground pepper, and let simmer, covered until the meat is tender. If using young lamb, 30 minutes will be sufficient; mutton may take up to 1 hour.

*continued overleaf*

Meanwhile, make the pie crust: Sift the flour and salt into a mixing bowl and make a hollow in the center. In a saucepan, combine the butter and water and bring to a boil. Pour the liquid into the hollow all at once and mix together quickly; beat until smooth. At first the dough will be too soft to handle, but as soon as it cools, roll out on a floured work surface about ⅛ to ¼ inch thick and use to line two 6-inch pie/tart pans, 1½ inches deep (or one 7-inch pie/tart pan to make one large pie). Keep back one-third of the dough for lids.

Preheat the oven to 425°F.

Fill the pastry shells with the meat mixture, which should be freshly cooked and slightly cooled. Brush the edges of the dough lightly with water and place the dough lids on top, pressing them tightly together. Roll out the dough scraps to make leaves or twirls to decorate the top of the pies; make a hole in the center. Brush the lids with beaten egg and then the decoration also.

Bake the pies for about 40 minutes, until the crust is well browned. Serve with a salad of fresh seasonal greens.

## VARIATION
— Puff pastry can be substituted for the hot water crust pie crust.

# BEEF WITH STOUT

Serves 6 to 8

Use your favorite stout for this recipe. In Cork we use Beamish or Murphy, but even Cork people have divided allegiances! Ireland now has a whole new generation of artisan and craft brewers—we've got quite the choice. Experiment with your local brew: Eight Degrees, Franciscan Well, Dungarvan—each gives the stew its own characteristic flavor.

2 pounds boneless stew beef, preferably marbled
   with fat, such as chuck or shank
seasoned all-purpose flour
3 tablespoons olive oil
2 onions, peeled and thinly sliced
½ cup Beamish, Murphy, or Guinness
1¾ cups beef stock
1 tablespoon granulated sugar
1 teaspoon English mustard powder

1 tablespoon Tomato Puree (page 18)
1 strip of dried orange peel
1 bouquet garni made up of 1 bay leaf, 1 thyme
   sprig, and 4 parsley stems
8 ounces portobello mushrooms
1 tablespoon salted butter
sea salt and freshly ground black pepper
coarsely chopped flat-leaf parsley, to garnish

Preheat the oven to 300°F.

Cut the meat into 1½-inch cubes and toss in the seasoned flour. In a hot sauté pan, heat some of the olive oil and brown the meat, in batches, on all sides. Transfer the meat to a Dutch oven. Add a bit more oil to the pan and cook the onions until nicely browned; deglaze with the stout. Transfer to the pot and add the stock, sugar, mustard, tomato puree, orange peel, and bouquet garni. Season with salt and freshly ground pepper. Bring to a boil, cover, and transfer to the oven to cook for 2 to 2½ hours or until the meat is tender.

Meanwhile, clean and slice the mushrooms. In a hot skillet, sauté the mushrooms in the butter. Season with salt and freshly ground pepper. Set aside.

When the stew is cooked, add the mushrooms and simmer on the stovetop for 2 to 3 minutes. Season to taste. Serve sprinkled with lots of chopped parsley.

This stew reheats well and improves with keeping for a day or two in the refrigerator. You may need to add more sugar to the recipe if you find it a slightly bitter from the stout.

# ITALIAN BEEF STEW

Serves 6 to 8

A super recipe for a beef stew, unusually it doesn't have pickled bacon or pickled pork, but you could add a few chunks. It's still a firm favorite after all these years, although we now serve it with some gremolata sprinkled over the top. Italian beef stew, like many other stews, is even better when served next day; it reheats deliciously over gentle heat on the stovetop or in a low oven and freezes brilliantly. Leftover stew, with or without any chunks of meat, makes a delicious sauce for pasta—just add a generous grating of Parmesan and some freshly chopped parsley

3 pounds dry-aged boneless beef chuck or
    lean flank
olive oil, for cooking
2 large carrots, peeled and cut into slices ½ inch
    thick
10 ounces onions, peeled and sliced
1 heaping tablespoon all-purpose flour
⅔ cup red wine
⅔ cup brown beef stock
1 cup Tomato Puree (page 18)

2 cups sliced mushrooms (portobello or
    meadow mushrooms have more flavor)
1 tablespoon freshly chopped flat-leaf parsley
sea salt and freshly ground black pepper
*For the gremolata*
¼ cup freshly chopped flat-leaf parsley
1 heaping teaspoon finely grated or finely chopped
    lemon zest
2 garlic cloves, finely chopped

Preheat the oven to 325°F.

Trim the meat of any excess fat, then cut into 1½-inch cubes. In a Dutch oven, heat 1 tablespoon of olive oil and sweat the carrots and onions over gentle heat with the lid on for 10 minutes. In a skillet, heat a bit more olive oil until almost smoking. Sear the pieces of meat on all sides, then reduce the heat, stir in the flour, and cook for 1 minute. Combine the wine, stock, and tomato puree and gradually add to the pot. Season with salt and freshly ground pepper. Cover and cook gently in the oven for 2 to 3 hours, depending on the cut of meat.

Meanwhile, in a hot skillet, sauté the mushrooms in a splash of olive oil and add to the pot with the chopped parsley about 30 minutes before the end of cooking.

Make the gremolata: In a small bowl, combine all the ingredients. Serve sprinkled over the stew with polenta, mashed potatoes, or noodles, and a good green salad.

# BOEUF BOURGUIGNON

Serves 6 to 8

A French classic. In Ireland, stew is generally regarded as something you feed to the family but not your honored guests. Not so in France, where this recipe for the most famous of all beef stews might be served for a special Sunday lunch or dinner with friends. After all it is not inexpensive to make: You need best-quality aged stew beef and the best part of a bottle of red wine. As the name suggests it used to be made with Burgundy, but with Burgundy prices nowadays, I think I might settle for using a good Beaujolais or a full-bodied Côtes du Rhône.

8 ounces slab bacon

1 to 2 tablespoons extra virgin olive oil

3 pounds dry-aged boneless beef chuck or
    lean flank, cut into 2-inch cubes

1 large carrot, peeled and sliced

6 ounces onions, peeled and sliced

2 tablespoons brandy (optional)

1¾ cups full-bodied red wine, such as Burgundy,
    Côtes du Rhône, or even a Beaujolais

1¼ to 1¾ cups brown beef stock

1 tablespoon tomato paste

2-inch piece of dried orange peel

1 thyme sprig

1 bay leaf

3 garlic cloves, peeled

18 to 24 pearl onions, depending on size

1 pound small portobello or meadow mushrooms,
    cut into quarters

Roux (optional—page 76)

sea salt and freshly ground black pepper

freshly chopped flat-leaf parsley, to garnish

Remove the rind from the bacon, then cut the bacon into 1½-inch cubes. If salty, blanch in a pot of boiling water, drain, and refresh in cold water. Dry well on paper towels. In a skillet, heat the olive oil and sauté the bacon until crisp and golden. Transfer the bacon to a Dutch oven.

Increase the heat so the oil and bacon fat are almost smoking. Dry off the meat with paper towels. Sauté, a few pieces at a time, until nicely browned on all sides, then add to the bacon. Toss the sliced carrot and onion in the remaining fat and add these also.

If there is any fat left in the pan at this stage, pour it off, add the brandy, if using, and carefully ignite with a long match, then deglaze the pan with the wine, scraping the bits of sediment on the pan until they dissolve. Bring to a boil and pour over the beef; this all adds to the flavor.

The casserole may be prepared ahead to this point. Let cool completely, cover, and refrigerate overnight, or at least for a few hours. The wine will have a tenderizing effect on the meat, and the other ingredients will add extra flavor as the meat marinates.

Later or the following day, add enough stock to almost cover the meat, the tomato paste, dried orange peel, thyme, bay leaf, and the whole garlic cloves. Season with salt and freshly ground pepper. Bring to a boil, cover, and simmer very gently either on the stovetop or in a preheated oven at 325°F until the meat is tender, 1½ to 2½ hours depending on the cut used. The meat should not fall apart but it should be tender enough to eat without too much chewing.

Meanwhile, prepare the pearl onions: Peel the onions—this task is made easier if you drop them in boiling water for 1 minute, run them under the cold faucet, trim, and then slip off the skins. Simmer gently in a small saucepan with about ½ inch of water or beef stock, covered with the pan lid—they will take 30 to 35 minutes depending on size. A knife should pierce them easily.

In a hot skillet, toss the mushrooms a few at a time in a splash of olive oil, then season with salt and freshly ground pepper.

When the meat is tender, pour the contents of the pot into a strainer or colander placed over a saucepan. Discard the herbs, carrot, onion, and dried orange peel. Return the meat to the pot with the pearl onions and mushrooms. Skim the fat from the liquid. There should be about 2½ cups of sauce. Pour into a saucepan, taste, and bring to a boil, then simmer. If the sauce is too thin or too weak, reduce for a few minutes, otherwise thicken slightly by whisking in a bit of roux. Pour over the meat, mushrooms, and onions and return to a boil, then simmer for a few minutes until heated through. Season to taste. Sprinkle with lots of chopped parsley and serve with a rich mashed potato.

Boeuf Bourguignon may be made a few days ahead and the flavor even improves with keeping for a day or two in the refrigerator.

# TRADITIONAL IRISH BACON
with cabbage & parsley sauce

Serves 12 to 15

Ireland's national dish of bacon and cabbage can be a sorry disappointment nowadays, partly because it is so difficult to get good-quality bacon with a decent bit of fat on it. Traditionally, the cabbage was always cooked in the bacon water. People could only hang one pot over the fire at a time, so when the bacon was almost cooked, they added the cabbage for the last 30 or 45 minutes of cooking. The bacon water gives a salty, unforgettable flavor, which many people, including me, still hanker for.

1 (about 7-pound) "collar bacon"—smoked pork shoulder (picnic shoulder)

1 Savoy or 2 pointed cabbages, cut into thin shreds

3½ tablespoons salted butter

freshly ground black pepper

*For the parsley sauce*

2½ cups whole milk

a few parsley stems

1 thyme sprig

a few slices of carrot (optional)

a few slices of onion (optional)

3½ tablespoons Roux (page 76)

¾ cup freshly chopped curly parsley

sea salt and freshly ground black pepper

In a stock pot, cover the meat in cold water and bring slowly to a boil. If very salty, there will be a white froth on top of the water, in which case discard the water and start again. Cover with hot water and the lid of the pan and simmer until almost cooked, 25 minutes per pound.

About 20 minutes before the end of cooking, add the shredded cabbage to the water in which the meat is boiling. Stir, cover, and continue to boil gently until both the cabbage and meat are tender, about 1¾ hours in total.

To make the parsley sauce, in a saucepan, combine the milk, herbs, and vegetables, if using. Bring the mixture to a simmer, season, and let simmer for 4 to 5 minutes. Strain the milk, bring it back to a boil, and whisk in the roux until the sauce is a light coating consistency. Season again with salt and freshly ground pepper. Add the chopped parsley and simmer on very low heat for 4 to 5 minutes. Season to taste.

Lift the meat onto a plate and remove the rind if desired. Strain the cabbage and discard the water (or, if it's not too salty, reserve it for a tomato soup). Add the butter to the cabbage and season with lots of ground pepper. Serve the meat with the cabbage, parsley sauce, and some boiled floury potatoes.

# SPICED LAMB with eggplant

A gorgeous, flavorful stew. It's worth doubling or even tripling the recipe, as it keeps and improves in the refrigerator for several days and freezes perfectly.

1 (2¼-pound) boneless shoulder of lamb

1 heaping teaspoon cumin seeds

3 eggplants

2 tablespoons extra virgin olive oil

7 ounces onions, peeled and sliced

1 large garlic clove, peeled and sliced

3 teaspoons freshly chopped mint

3 teaspoons freshly chopped sweet marjoram

14 ounces very ripe tomatoes or 1 (14½-ounce) can
   diced tomatoes

sea salt and freshly ground black pepper

cilantro leaves, to garnish

Preheat the oven to 350°F.

Cut the meat into 1-inch cubes. In a skillet, dry-roast the cumin seeds for a few minutes. Using a pestle and mortar, crush the seeds and sprinkle over the meat. Cut the eggplants into larger cubes than the meat. Sprinkle with salt, put into a colander with a plate on top to weigh them down, and let drain.

In a sauté pan, heat the olive oil and sweat the sliced onion and garlic. Add the meat and let it to color, sprinkle with the chopped mint and marjoram, and season with salt and freshly ground pepper. Transfer to a Dutch oven, cover, and put into the oven.

Rinse the eggplants and drain, then dry them with paper towels. Toss them in the olive oil in the sauté pan, season with salt and freshly ground pepper, and let color. Add to the meat in the Dutch oven, stir, and replace the lid.

Meanwhile, peel the fresh tomatoes, if using, and add them to the meat mixture in the pot. Season with salt and freshly ground pepper. Replace the lid and continue cooking until the meat is meltingly tender, about 30 minutes. Season to taste.

Degrease the cooking liquid if necessary. Garnish with lots of cilantro leaves and serve with rice pilaf or homemade fettuccine.

# BEEF TENDERLOIN with mushrooms & thyme

Serves 6

Always a treat, this is super rich and delicious—you can alter the proportion of stock to cream if you'd prefer a less unctuous sauce, but the original is wonderful.

1 (2¼-pound) dry-aged beef tenderloin roast

1 tablespoon butter

2 teaspoons extra virgin olive oil

sea salt, freshly ground black pepper, and
   granulated sugar

watercress, chervil, or flat-leaf parsley sprigs,
   to garnish

*For the sauce*

2 tablespoons salted butter

3 tablespoons finely chopped shallots or scallions

3¼ cups sliced white button mushrooms

⅔ cup red wine

⅔ cup brown beef stock

1¼ cups light cream

Roux (optional—page 76)

1 teaspoon thyme leaves

a few drops of lemon juice

Make the sauce: In a skillet, melt the butter and sweat the shallots or scallions over gentle heat until soft but not colored; remove from the pan. Increase the heat and sauté the mushrooms a few at a time, seasoning each batch and adding to the shallots or scallions as soon as they are cooked. Add the wine and stock to the pan and boil rapidly until the liquid has reduced to about ⅓ cup. Add the cream and let simmer for a few minutes to thicken (whisk in a tiny bit of roux if desired). Add the sautéed mushroom and onion mixture and the thyme leaves. Simmer for 1 to 2 minutes; do not let the sauce thicken too much or it will be heavy and cloying. Correct the seasoning if necessary. If the sauce tastes a bit too rich, add some water along with the lemon juice. This sauce can be cooked several hours in advance and reheated just before serving.

Prepare the beef: Trim the meat of any fat or membrane and cut into 2-ounce pieces. In a hot skillet, melt the butter with the olive oil. When the foam subsides, sauté the beef. Remember not to overcrowd the pan; the pieces of beef will only take 1 to 3 minutes each side, depending on how you like it cooked. As soon as the beef is cooked, transfer the pieces to an upturned plate resting on a larger plate to catch any drippings.

To serve, reheat the sauce, serve three pieces of steak per person on individual plates or on a large serving plate, and coat with the hot mushroom sauce. Garnish with watercress, chervil, or flat-leaf parsley sprigs.

# fish & seafood

# MACKEREL WITH MUSHROOMS & HERBS

Serves 4

My father-in-law, Ivan Allen, had a mushroom farm in Shanagarry for many years. This was his favorite way to eat the beautiful mackerel fresh from the little day-boats in Ballycotton. This mushroom, garlic, and herb mixture is also delicious served with sautéed chicken livers on toast as an appetizer.

4 very fresh whole mackerel, cleaned

seasoned all-purpose flour, for coating

1 tablespoon clarified butter (page 185), plus more if needed

4 ounces portobello or meadow mushrooms, sliced

1 to 2 garlic cloves, crushed

4 teaspoons finely chopped fresh herbs, such as thyme, parsley, chives, fennel, and lemon balm, plus more to garnish

sea salt and freshly ground black pepper

Fillet the mackerel, then wash, dry well with paper towels, and dip in seasoned flour to coat. In a skillet large enough to fit the fish in a single layer, melt the butter and sauté the fish until golden on both sides, 4 to 5 minutes each side.

Remove the fish to a hot serving dish or four individual plates. Add the mushrooms and garlic to the pan with a bit more butter if necessary. Cook over high heat for 2 to 3 minutes, add the chopped fresh herbs, and season with a little salt and freshly ground pepper if necessary. Serve this mixture as a garnish down the center of each fish and sprinkle with extra chopped herbs.

# BALLYCOTTON FISH PIE

Serves 6 to 8

How fortunate are we to live close to the little fishing village of Ballycotton in East Cork. Everyone loves fish pie and the combination I use depends on the fish catch. Omit mussels and shrimp if they are not available. This dish may be served in individual dishes: Scallop shells are particularly attractive, are completely oven-safe, and may be used over and over again.

2½ pounds cod, haddock, hake, or grey sea mullet
    fillets, or a mixture
1 tablespoon salted butter
2½ cups whole milk
4 ounces cooked shelled mussels
4 ounces cooked and peeled small shrimp
3½ tablespoons Roux (page 76)
¼ teaspoon mustard, preferably Dijon

1¼ to 1½ cups shredded Irish Cheddar cheese or
    heaping ¾ cup grated Parmesan cheese
2 tablespoons freshly chopped parsley
3¼ cups fluffy mashed potato or champ (optional)
sea salt and freshly ground black pepper
*For the buttered crumbs*
2 tablespoons salted butter
1 cup fresh white bread crumbs

Preheat the oven to 350°F.

Skin the fish and cut into portions: 6 ounces for a main course, 3 ounces for an appetizer. Season with salt and freshly ground pepper. Grease a sauté pan with the butter, lay the pieces of fish in it, and cover with the milk. Bring to a boil, then simmer until the fish has changed color, 4 to 5 minutes. Remove the fish to a serving dish or dishes with a slotted spoon. Scatter the mussels and shrimp over the top.

Bring the milk back to a boil and thicken with roux to a light coating consistency. Add the mustard, two-thirds of the cheese, and the parsley. Reserve the remaining cheese for sprinkling over the top. Season well with salt and freshly ground pepper.

Next make the buttered crumbs: In a skillet, melt the butter and stir in the bread crumbs. Remove from the heat immediately and let cool.

Coat the fish with the sauce. Pipe fluffy mashed potato or champ in swirls on top for a more substantial dish, if desired. Mix the remaining cheese with the buttered crumbs and sprinkle over the top.

Bake for 15 to 20 minutes or until the fish pie is heated through and the top is golden brown and crispy. If necessary, place the fish pie under a broiler to brown the edge of the potato, 1 to 2 minutes, before you serve.

# BAKED SUMMER PLAICE with herb butter

A Ballymaloe classic, this simple cooking technique can be used not only for baking plaice and sole but for all very fresh flat fish, such as turbot, flounder, and lemon sole. Because it's cooked whole on the bone, it retains maximum flavor. Peel the skin off the top when cooked and coat with a simple herb butter, hollandaise, or beurre blanc sauce. We sometimes add a few peeled shrimp, mussels, cockles (substitute small clams), or periwinkles to the butter or sauce for an even more exquisite dish.

4 very fresh summer whole plaice or Dover sole, cleaned

sea salt and freshly ground black pepper

*For the herb butter*

3½ tablespoons to ½ cup (1 stick) salted butter

4 teaspoons mixed finely chopped fresh flat-leaf parsley, chives, fennel, and thyme leaves

Preheat the oven to 375°F.

Turn the fish on its side and remove the head. Wash the fish and clean the slit very thoroughly. With a sharp knife, cut through the dark skin right round the fish, just where the "fringe" meets the flesh. Be careful to cut neatly and to cross the side cuts at the tail or it will be difficult to remove the skin later on.

Sprinkle the fish with salt and freshly ground pepper. In a shallow baking pan, lay the fish in a generous ¼ inch of water. Bake for 20 to 30 minutes, depending on the size of the fish. The water should have almost evaporated as the fish is cooked. Check to see whether the fish is cooked by lifting the flesh from the bone at the head and it should lift off the bone easily and be white with no trace of pink.

Just before serving, make the herb butter: In a saucepan, gently melt the butter, then stir in the freshly chopped herbs.

To serve, grasp the skin near the tail of the fish and pull it off gently (the skin will tear badly if not properly cut as above). Lift the fish onto hot plates and spoon the herb butter evenly over the fish. Serve immediately.

# MONKFISH with cucumber & dill weed hollandaise

Serves 4 or
8 as an
appetizer

Even though its appearance is ugly, monkfish is one of the most sought-after fish, firm and succulent with no tiny bones to worry about. What's not to love about monkfish served with hollandaise?

1 tablespoon salt

1½ pounds monkfish tail, cut into slices
    ½ inch thick

dill weed sprigs and dill weed flowers if in season,
    to garnish

*For the cucumber & dill weed hollandaise*

2 large organic, free-range egg yolks

2 teaspoons cold water

½ cup (1 stick) salted butter, diced, plus
    ½ tablespoon

about 1 teaspoon freshly squeezed lemon juice

⅓ cucumber, peeled and cut into tiny dice

1 tablespoon freshly chopped dill weed

First make the hollandaise sauce: Put the egg yolks in a heavy, stainless steel saucepan over very low heat or in a heat-safe bowl over hot water. Add the cold water and beat thoroughly. Add the ½ cup (1 stick) butter a piece at a time, whisking continuously. As soon as one piece melts, add the next piece. The mixture will gradually thicken, but if it shows signs of becoming too thick or slightly scrambling, immediately remove from the heat and add a splash of cold water if necessary. Do not leave the pan or stop whisking until the sauce is made. Finally, add the lemon juice to taste. If the sauce is slow to thicken, it may be because you are too cautious and the heat is too low. Increase the heat slightly and continue to whisk until the sauce thickens to a light coating consistency. Pour into a bowl and keep warm.

In a saucepan, melt the remaining ½ tablespoon butter and toss the cucumber in it for 1 to 2 minutes. Add to the hollandaise sauce with the freshly chopped dill weed.

Just before serving, in a large pot, bring 2½ quarts of water to a boil and add the salt. Add the monkfish pieces and bring back to a boil, then simmer until the pieces are no longer opaque but completely white and tender, 4 to 5 minutes. Drain the monkfish thoroughly.

To serve, arrange overlapping pieces of monkfish on individual plates. If the hollandaise sauce is too thick, whisk in a bit of hot water—it should be a light coating consistency. Spoon carefully over the fish. Garnish with feathery dill weed and dill weed flowers in season. Serve immediately.

# COD, HADDOCK, OR HAKE
## with leeks & buttered crumbs

Serves 6 or 12 as
a starter

The gentle flavor of buttered leeks is particularly good with fish, but the basic recipe with mornay sauce and crunchy crumbs always gets a brilliant reaction. Sautéed mushrooms, tomato fondue, or peperonata also complement the flavor of the fish instead of leeks.

2½ pounds cod, haddock, hake, grey sea mullet,
    or pollock
1 tablespoon salted butter
sea salt and freshly ground black pepper
*For the mornay sauce*
2½ cups whole milk
a few slices of carrot and onion
3 to 4 black peppercorns
1 thyme and 1 parsley sprig
3½ tablespoons Roux (page 76)
¼ teaspoon Dijon mustard

1⅓ to 1½ cups shredded Cheddar cheese or
    ¾ cup grated Parmesan cheese
1 to 2 tablespoons chopped parsley (optional)
*For the buttered leeks*
2 tablespoons salted butter
1 pound leeks, halved and sliced into rounds
    ¼ inch thick
*For the buttered crumbs*
2 tablespoons butter
1 cup fresh white bread crumbs

First make the mornay sauce: In a saucepan, combine the milk, carrot and onion, peppercorns, and herbs. Bring to a boil, then simmer for 4 to 5 minutes. Remove from the heat and let infuse for 10 minutes. Strain out the vegetables, bring the milk back to a boil, and thicken with the roux to a coating consistency. Remove from the heat and let cool for 1 minute, then add the mustard and two-thirds of the cheese, reserving the remainder for sprinkling over the top. Season to taste. Add the parsley, if using.

Make the buttered leeks: In a heavy-bottom saucepan, melt the butter. When it foams, add the leeks and toss gently to coat with the butter. Season with salt and freshly ground pepper. Cover with a wax paper lid and a close-fitting lid. Reduce the heat and cook the leeks very gently for until semisoft and moist, 8 to 10 minutes.

Next make the buttered crumbs: In a skillet, melt the butter and stir in the bread crumbs. Immediately remove from the heat and let cool.

Preheat the oven to 350°F. Skin the fish and cut into portions: 6 ounces for a main course, 3 ounces for an appetizer. Season with salt and freshly ground pepper. Grease a baking dish with the butter and cover the bottom of the dish with a layer of the buttered leeks. Coat with some mornay sauce, lay the fish on top, and coat with more sauce. Mix the remaining cheese with the buttered crumbs and sprinkle over the top. Bake for 25 to 30 minutes or until the fish is cooked through and the top is golden brown and crispy.

# MOULES PROVENÇALE

Serves 6 to 8

Mussels, although available year round in Ireland, are at their plumpest and best in the colder months of the year. They are terrifically good value in comparison to other shellfish, very versatile, and a perennial favorite. Do not skimp on the garlic in this recipe or they will taste rather dull and "bready." You can also use this recipe with manila clams, which grow off the West Cork coast of Ireland, around Kenmare Bay.

about 3½ to 4 pounds fresh mussels

*For the Provençale butter*

2 large garlic cloves

2 tablespoons finely chopped flat-leaf parsley

1 tablespoon extra virgin olive oil

5 tablespoons salted butter, softened

fresh white bread crumbs

Check that all the mussels are closed. If any are open, tap the mussel on the work surface, and if they do not close within a few seconds, discard. (The rule with shellfish is always, "If in doubt, throw it out.") Scrape off any barnacles from the mussel shells. Wash the mussels well in several changes of cold water. Then spread them in a single layer in a large saucepan, cover with a folded kitchen towel or a lid, and cook over gentle heat until the shells open. This usually takes 2 to 3 minutes—the mussels are cooked just as soon as the shells pop open. Remove them from the pan immediately or they will shrink and toughen.

Remove the beard (the little tuft of coarse "hair"that attached the mussel to the rock or rope it grew on). Discard one shell. Loosen the mussel from the other shell, but let it stay in the shell. Let cool completely.

Meanwhile, make the Provençale butter: Peel and crush the garlic cloves. Using a pestle and mortar, pound the garlic with the finely chopped parsley and extra virgin olive oil. Gradually beat in the butter (this may be done either in a bowl with a spoon or in a blender or food processor). Spread the soft garlic butter evenly over the mussels in the shells and dip each one into the bread crumbs. They may be prepared ahead to this point and frozen in a covered box lined with plastic wrap or parchment paper.

Brown under a broiler and serve with crusty white bread to mop up the delicious garlicky juices.

### VARIATION

*Mussels with Wild Garlic (Ramps) or Watercress Butter* Substitute wild garlic (ramps) or watercress leaves for parsley in the above recipe.

# THREE-MINUTE FISH

Serves 4

This is the fastest fish recipe I know and certainly one of the most delicious. It can be fun to mix pink- and white-fleshed fish on the same plate, such as salmon and sea bass.

We also love crudo—just lay slices of super fresh fish on a chilled plate. Drizzle freshly squeezed lemon and some extra virgin olive oil over the top and maybe a sprinkle of fresh chervil sprigs.

1 pound very fresh fish fillet, such as
   wild salmon, cod, turbot, large sole, sea bass,
   or grey sea mullet
extra virgin olive oil or melted butter

finely chopped fresh herbs such as parsley, thyme,
   chives, and chervil
sea salt and freshly ground black pepper

Season the fish fillet with salt and freshly ground pepper about 30 minutes before cutting, then refrigerate the fish to stiffen it.

Preheat the oven to 450°F.

While the oven is heating, lightly brush four oven-safe plates with extra virgin olive oil or melted butter. Put the fish fillet on a cutting board skin side down; cut the flesh into slices scant ¼ inch thick down onto the skin. Arrange the slices on the bottom of the oven-safe plates, but do not let them overlap or they will cook unevenly. Brush the fish slices with more olive oil or melted butter, season with salt and freshly ground pepper, and sprinkle each plate with some freshly chopped herbs. Bake for 3 minutes; you might like to check after 2 minutes if the slices are exceptionally thin. The fish is cooked when it looks opaque.

Rush the fish to the table and serve with crusty white bread, a good green salad, and a glass of white wine.

### VARIATION
Ring the changes with a bit of chopped chili, cilantro, or freshly roasted crushed spices, such as cumin or coriander.

# PENNE WITH FRESH SALMON & green peas

Serves 4

Sanford Allen, a charismatic American violinist friend, gave me this fresh-tasting pasta recipe originally. Ideally use fresh peas, but good-quality frozen peas also work well. Sometimes I omit the lemon juice and add a good dash of cream instead.

2⅓ cups dry penne

1¾ cups peas

8 ounces fresh wild or organic farmed salmon fillet, or half smoked and half fresh salmon

3 tablespoons extra virgin olive oil

1 large garlic clove, finely chopped

pinch of granulated sugar

1 tablespoon salted butter, melted

2 to 3 tablespoons freshly chopped dill weed and flat-leaf parsley, plus more to garnish

freshly squeezed juice of ½ lemon

sea salt and freshly ground black pepper

In a large pot, bring 4¼ quarts of water to a boil with 2 tablespoons of salt. Add the penne and cook until al dente, 10 to 12 minutes.

Meanwhile, in a saucepan of boiling water, blanch the peas for 2 to 3 minutes, then drain. Frozen peas may take a minute more to cook.

Skin the salmon and cut into ½-inch cubes, removing any pin bones. In a sauté pan, heat 1 tablespoon of the olive oil, add the garlic, and toss over medium heat for a minute or two. Add the salmon and toss gently until it changes color. Stir in the blanched peas. Season with the sugar, salt, and freshly ground pepper.

Drain the penne, return to the pot, and toss in the remaining olive oil and the melted butter. Add the salmon mixture, herbs, and freshly squeezed lemon juice, toss gently, and season to taste. Transfer to a hot serving dish, sprinkle with lots of chopped dill weed and parsley, and enjoy immediately.

# SMOKED & FRESH SALMON FISH CAKES
## with parsley butter

Serves 10

Fish cakes and fish pie make the yummiest suppers. Here, I'm using both fresh and smoked salmon, but of course you can use a variety of other fish. A big dollop of tartare sauce or aioli is pretty irresistible too.

10 ounces fresh salmon fillet

1 pound unpeeled potatoes, such as
    russet or Idaho

1 large organic, free-range egg, beaten, plus more
    beaten egg for coating

2 to 3½ tablespoons salted butter

1 tablespoon freshly chopped parsley

2 tablespoons freshly chopped cilantro

2 tablespoons chopped scallions

2 ounces smoked salmon, cut into
    ⅛-inch cubes

creamy milk (optional)

well-seasoned all-purpose flour

fresh white bread crumbs or panko crumbs

extra virgin olive oil or clarified butter (page 185),
    for cooking

sea salt and freshly ground black pepper

*For the parsley butter*

3½ tablespoons butter

4 teaspoons finely chopped parsley

a few drops of freshly squeezed lemon juice

Make the parsley butter: In a mixing bowl, cream the butter and stir in the parsley and the lemon juice a drop or two at a time. Roll into butter pats or form into a roll and wrap in wax paper or aluminum foil, twisting each end so that it looks like a cracker. Refrigerate to harden.

In a saucepan, cook the salmon in boiling salted water, 5 to 8 minutes depending on the thickness of the fish. Let cool, then remove the skin and any pin bones. Flake the salmon.

Meanwhile, in another saucepan, boil the potatoes in their skins until tender. Drain and let cool. When cool enough to handle, peel off the skin and mash right away. Add the beaten egg, butter, chopped herbs, scallions, flaked fresh salmon, and diced smoked salmon. Season with plenty of salt and freshly ground pepper, adding a bit of creamy milk if the mixture is too stiff.

Shape into patties about 3 inches in diameter and 1 inch thick. Dip first in well-seasoned flour, then the beaten egg for coating, and finally in bread crumbs.

In a skillet, heat some extra virgin olive oil or clarified butter over gentle heat. Cook the salmon and potato patties until golden on one side, flip over, and cook on the other side for 4 to 5 minutes; they should be crusty and golden.

Serve on hot plates with a pat or slice of parsley butter melting on top, or a dollop of homemade tartare sauce or aioli (page 32).

# SMOKED HADDOCK WITH PARMESAN

Serves 6

Seek out an artisan smoked product or try smoking your own fish at home—it's so easy and such fun. If you surround the fish with some mashed potato, supper's ready. Follow with a salad of organic greens.

1½ pounds finnan haddie (smoked haddock) fillet

2½ cups whole milk

a few slices of carrot

a few slices of onion

1 bouquet garni

3½ tablespoons Roux (page 76)

2 tablespoons freshly chopped parsley

1 heaping cup grated Parmesan cheese, or
    use 1 cup shredded sharp cheddar

Buttered Crumbs (page 96)

4 cups mashed potato

Preheat the oven to 350°F.

Cut the smoked fish into portions weighing 2 to 4 ounces and arrange in a wide sauté pan.

In a saucepan, combine the milk, carrot, onion, and bouquet garni. Bring slowly to a boil, then simmer for 3 to 4 minutes. Remove from the heat and let infuse for 10 to 15 minutes. Strain. Cover the fish with the flavoured milk and simmer until just cooked, 3 to 6 minutes depending on the thickness of the fish. Using a slotted spoon, transfer the fish to an oven-safe serving dish.

Bring the milk back to a boil and thicken with the roux to a light coating consistency. Add the parsley and half the cheese, then spoon over the fish in the dish. Sprinkle with a mixture of buttered crumbs and the remaining cheese. Pipe mashed potato around the outside of the dish. (You can prepare ahead to this point.)

Bake for 15 to 20 minutes or until the top is crisp and bubbly and the potato edges are golden.

# COD, HADDOCK, OR HAKE
with Dijon mustard sauce

Serves 6

Virtually any round fish may be used in this recipe, so you could also use grey sea mullet or pollock. This recipe is another gem that you'll return to over and over again.

3½ tablespoons salted butter

1½ cups chopped onions

2 pounds fresh cod, haddock, or hake fillets

2½ cups whole milk

3½ tablespoons heavy whipping cream

¼ cup all-purpose flour

2 to 3 tablespoons Dijon or English mustard

1 tablespoon freshly chopped parsley

sea salt and freshly ground black pepper

In a saucepan, melt the butter and sweat the onions, covered, until golden brown.

Skin the fish if necessary and cut into portions. Season with salt and freshly ground pepper. Put into a wide sauté pan or skillet, cover with the milk and cream, and bring to a boil, then simmer gently for 4 to 6 minutes, depending on the thickness of the fish. Remove the fish carefully to a serving dish.

Add the flour to the onions, stir, and cook for 2 minutes. Add in the hot fishy milk and bring back to a boil, then simmer until a light coating consistency, 3 to 4 minutes. Add the mustard and chopped parsley, season to taste, then pour over the fish and serve with your choice of vegetables.

You can leave the dish to cool and refrigerate, then reheat later in a preheated oven at 350°F for about 20 minutes.

## VARIATIONS

⌐ Sprinkle 1½ to 2⅓ cups sliced mushrooms, sautéed, over or under the fish before saucing.

⌐ In a covered saucepan, sweat 1 pound of finely sliced leeks in 2 tablespoons of salted butter over gentle heat and use instead of mushrooms.

⌐ Peel and chop 3 to 4 ounces cucumber. In a covered saucepan, sweat the cucumber in 1 to 2 tablespoons of salted butter with 2 teaspoons of chopped dill weed over gentle heat. Use instead of mushrooms and omit mustard from the sauce.

⌐ Put a layer of Tomato Fondue (page 127) on or over the fish and proceed as in the master recipe (omit mustard from the sauce).

⌐ Put a layer of peperonata under or over the fish and proceed as in the master recipe (omit mustard from the sauce).

# vegetables

# ASPARAGUS & SCALLION TART

Serves 6

In Ireland asparagus is in season for one month only, during May. But even if you can get it year round, it's simply not worth making this tart unless fresh spring asparagus is available. The tart shell needs to be well cooked before the filling is added.

*For the crust*

¾ cup plus 2 tablespoons all-purpose flour

3½ tablespoons salted butter

1 small organic, free-range egg (optional),
   plus more beaten egg to glaze

*For the filling*

1 tablespoon salted butter

1 tablespoon extra virgin olive oil

9 ounces onions, peeled and finely chopped
   (I use about half scallion complete with
    green tops and half white onion)

5 ounces asparagus, trimmed and ends peeled

3 large organic, free-range eggs

⅓ cup plus 2 tablespoons heavy whipping cream

1 cup shredded Cheddar cheese

sea salt and freshly ground black pepper

Preheat the oven to 350°F.

First make the crust: Sift the flour into a mixing bowl. Cut in the butter using a pastry cutter or by pinching the fat into the flour with your fingertips until the mixture resembles coarse bread crumbs. Mix in enough water or the egg beaten with a small amount of water to bind the dough; be careful not to make it too sticky. Wrap in plastic wrap and refrigerate for 15 minutes.

On a floured work surface, roll out the dough into a circle large enough (no more than ⅛ inch thick) to line a 7-inch quiche/tart pan. Line the tart shell with wax paper and fill to the top with pie weights or dried beans. Bake blind on a lower rack for about 20 minutes. Remove the pie weights and paper, brush the bottom with the beaten egg, and return to the oven for 3 to 4 minutes. This seals the dough and helps to avoid a "soggy bottom."

Next make the filling: In a sauté pan, melt the butter, add the olive oil and chopped onions, and sweat with a good pinch of salt until soft but not colored.

In a wide saucepan, cook the asparagus in boiling salted water until al dente, 3 to 4 minutes, then drain. Refresh in cold water and drain again. When cool enough to handle, cut into ½-inch pieces. In a mixing bowl, beat the eggs, then add the cream, sweated onion, almost all of the cheese, and the cooked asparagus (reserve a few of the tips to arrange on top, if desired. Season with salt and freshly ground pepper.

Pour the filling into the tart shell, sprinkle the remaining cheese on top, and bake for 40 to 45 minutes or until a toothpick inserted into the center just comes out clean. Serve warm, with a good green salad.

# ZUCCHINI & BASIL LASAGNA

Serves 6 to 8

When you consider that making lasagna is just a technique, then you can ring the changes with all manner of fillings. This simple vegetarian version is unexpectedly delicious. I sometimes use sweet marjoram instead of basil with equally tasty results.

9 lasagna noodles (choose the thinnest lasagna noodles available)

2 pounds zucchini, thinly sliced and cooked for 3 to 4 minutes in extra virgin olive oil

1½ cups freshly grated Parmesan cheese, preferably Parmigiano Reggiano

20 to 30 basil leaves, depending on size, plus more to garnish

sea salt and freshly ground black pepper

*For the béchamel sauce*

3¾ cups whole milk

a few slices of carrot

a few slices of onion

3 small thyme sprigs

3 small parsley sprigs

9 black peppercorns

7 tablespoons Roux (page 76)

Preheat the oven to 350°F.

In a large pot, blanch the lasagna in boiling salted water for a minute or so if it is homemade, or according to the directions on the package. Drain and lay on a kitchen towel until needed.

Make the béchamel sauce: In a saucepan, combine the milk, carrot, onion, peppercorns, thyme, and parsley. Bring to a boil, then simmer for 4 to 5 minutes. Remove from the heat and let infuse for 10 minutes.

Strain out the vegetables and herbs, bring the milk back to a boil, and whisk in the roux to thicken to a light coating consistency. Let bubble gently for 4 to 5 minutes. Season to taste.

Taste the cooked zucchini and ensure they are delicious and well seasoned. Grease a 10 x 12-inch gratin dish. Spread some of the béchamel sauce on the bottom of the dish and sprinkle with some of the grated Parmesan. Cover with three lasagna noodles, more béchamel sauce, a sprinkling of Parmesan, half the zucchini, and a layer of basil leaves. Next add another layer of lasagna noodles and repeat the previous layer. Add the final layer of noodles and cover with the remaining sauce and a good sprinkling of Parmesan. (Ensure all the noodles are coated with the sauce.)

Bake for 10 to 15 minutes or until golden and bubbly on top. If possible, let stand for 5 to 10 minutes before cutting so the layers compact. Serve garnished with more basil leaves and a good green salad.

# PIZZA with broccoli, mozzarella & garlic

Makes 1
Serves 1 to 2

Philip Dennhardt launched the pop-up Saturday Pizzas at the Ballymaloe Cookery School in 2008 and quickly gained a cult following. I find it convenient to pop a few rolled-out uncooked pizza crusts in the freezer when using this dough. You can take one out, put the topping on, and slide it straight in the oven. What could be easier! This dough also makes delicious white yeast bread, which you can shape into rolls, loaves, and braids.

semolina flour, to sprinkle

2 tablespoons extra virgin olive oil

2 to 3 garlic cloves, cut into thin slivers

4 ounces calabrese (green sprouting broccoli), broccoli, broccolini, or romanesco, cooked

3 ounces buffalo mozzarella, torn

2½ tablespoons grated Parmesan or aged Coolea cheese

flaky sea salt

chili oil (optional)

*For the pizza dough*

5 cups unbleached bread flour or 4⅓ cups unbleached bread flour and 1 cup rye flour

2 teaspoons salt

1 heaping tablespoon granulated sugar

3½ tablespoons butter

1 (¼-ounce) package quick-rise yeast

2 to 4 tablespoons olive oil, plus more for brushing

about 2 cups lukewarm water, more if necessary

Make the dough: Sift the flour into a large, wide mixing bowl and add the salt and sugar. Cut in the butter using a pastry cutter or by pinching the fat into the flour with your fingertips, add the yeast, and mix together thoroughly. Make a hollow in the center of the dry ingredients and add the oil and most of the lukewarm water. Gradually combine to form a loose dough. You can add more water or flour if needed. Turn the dough onto a lightly floured work surface, cover, and let relax for about 5 minutes.

Knead the dough until smooth and springy, 8 to 9 minutes by hand or 5 minutes using a stand mixer fitted with a dough hook. Let the dough relax again for about 10 minutes, then divide and shape into eight equal balls of dough, each weighing about 5 ounces. Lightly brush the balls of dough with olive oil. If you have time, put the oiled balls of dough into a plastic bag and chill in the refrigerator, which makes the dough easier to handle, but it can be used immediately.

Preheat the oven to 475°F and put in a baking sheet to heat up.

On a well-floured work surface, roll out a ball of dough to a 10-inch circle. Sprinkle a little semolina all over the surface of a pizza paddle, if using, and sit the pizza crust on top.

Brush the edges of the crust with extra virgin olive oil. Sprinkle thin slivers of garlic over the crust, arrange the broccoli florets on top, and sprinkle over the cheese. Drizzle with extra virgin olive oil and season with flaky sea salt. Slide off the paddle onto the hot baking sheet and bake for 5 to 8 minutes. Drizzle with chili oil if desired and serve immediately.

# SUMMER HEIRLOOM TOMATO & BASIL TART

Serves 6 to 8

This tart is only sublime when the tomatoes are superbly ripe and the basil is in season, otherwise it's probably better to make something else. I love it made with a mixture of the heirloom tomatoes we grow in the greenhouse, but any variety of ripe, juicy red ones will be good too.

*For the crust*

1⅓ cups plus 1 tablespoon all-purpose flour

5 tablespoons salted butter

1 large organic, free-range egg yolk

2 tablespoons water

*For the filling*

2 large organic, free-range eggs

⅓ cup heavy whipping cream

¾ cup shredded Emmental or Gruyère cheese

¼ cup freshly grated Parmesan cheese, preferably Parmigiano Reggiano

10 ounces very ripe heirloom tomatoes

pinch of granulated sugar

dash of balsamic vinegar (optional)

4 to 5 large basil leaves, torn

1 tablespoon finely snipped chives

sea salt and freshly ground black pepper

Preheat the oven to 350°F.

First make the crust: Sift the flour into a wide mixing bowl. Cut in the butter using a pastry cutter or by pinching the fat into the flour with your fingertips until the mixture resembles coarse bread crumbs. Beat together the egg yolk and water, then mix into the dough mixture to bind. Add a touch more water if necessary, but do not make the dough too sticky. Wrap in plastic wrap and refrigerate for 15 minutes.

On a floured work surface, roll out the dough into a circle large enough (about ⅛ inch thick) to line a 8-inch quiche/tart pan. Line with wax paper and fill to the top with pie weights or dried beans. Let rest for 15 minutes and then bake for 20 minutes. Remove the pie weights and paper and let cool.

Next make the filling: In a mixing bowl, beat the eggs with the cream, then add the cheese and season with salt and freshly ground pepper to taste. Drop the tomatoes into boiling water for about 30 seconds, then transfer to ice water to cool slightly. Peel off the skin and cut into rings ¼ inch thick. Season with the sugar, salt, freshly ground pepper, and balsamic vinegar if you have a nice bottle to hand. Put a few tablespoons of the filling into the tart shell and then a layer of tomato rings. Sprinkle on a layer of basil and chives. Spoon in the remaining filling and top with the remaining seasoned tomato rings. Sprinkle with a few flakes of sea salt.

Bake for about 30 minutes or until the tart is just set and golden on top. Serve with a salad of organic greens.

# MAC 'N' CHEESE

What's not to love about mac 'n' cheese? It's just about everyone's favorite comfort food. Gorgeous in its original form, but you can vary it almost infinitely—lobster mac 'n' cheese, or add smoked mackerel, eel, or salmon, or just some bacon.

2 cups dry macaroni

3½ tablespoons salted butter

6 tablespoons all-purpose flour

3½ cups whole milk, boiling

¼ teaspoon Dijon or English mustard

1 tablespoon freshly chopped flat-leaf parsley
  (optional)

1⅓ cups shredded sharp Cheddar cheese, or a
  mixture of Gruyère, Parmesan, and Cheddar,
  plus ¼ cup for sprinkling on top

sea salt and freshly ground black pepper

In a large pot, bring 3½ quarts of water to a boil and add 2 teaspoons of salt. Sprinkle in the macaroni and stir to ensure it doesn't stick together. Cook until just tender, 10 to 15 minutes. Drain well.

Meanwhile, in a saucepan, melt the butter, add the flour, and cook over medium heat, stirring occasionally, for 1 to 2 minutes. Remove from the heat. Gradually whisk in the milk, then return to a boil, stirring continuously. Add the mustard, parsley, if using, and cheese, and season with salt and freshly ground pepper to taste. Add the cooked macaroni, bring back to a boil, and season to taste. Mac 'n' cheese reheats very successfully provided the pasta is not overcooked in the first place.

Turn into a 1-quart pie dish and sprinkle the ¼ cup cheese over the top. Reheat in a preheated oven at 350°F for 15 to 20 minutes. It is very good served with cold meat, particularly ham.

## VARIATIONS

*Mac 'n' Cheese with Smoked Salmon or Smoked Mackerel* Add 8 ounces smoked salmon or smoked mackerel, diced, to the mac 'n' cheese.

*Mac 'n' Cheese with Mushrooms & Zucchini* Add 3 cups sliced mushrooms, sautéed, and 1½ cups sliced zucchini, cooked in olive oil with a bit of garlic and sweet marjoram or basil, to the mac 'n' cheese. Toss gently, turn into a hot serving dish, and scatter with shredded cheese—delish.

*Mac 'n' Cheese with Chorizo* Add scant 2 cups diced cured Spanish chorizo and lots of chopped parsley to the mac 'n' cheese as you put it into the dish.

# GRATIN OF LEEKS MORNAY

Serves 8

A comforting supper dish, I sometimes wrap each leek in a slice of ham before coating in the mornay sauce, as Maman did when I was an au pair in France. Belgian endive may be substituted for leeks, and very delicious they are too.

8 leeks
2½ cups whole milk
a few slices of carrot and onion
5 black peppercorns
5 to 7 tablespoons Roux (page 76)
1 thyme and 1 parsley sprig

¼ teaspoon Dijon mustard
1¼ to 1½ cups shredded Cheddar cheese or
    heaping ¾ cup grated Parmesan cheese
Buttered Crumbs (page 96—optional)
sea salt and freshly ground black pepper

Preheat the oven to 350°F.

Trim most of the green parts off the leeks (reserve for making stock). Keep the white parts whole, slit the top, and wash well under cold running water. In a covered saucepan, cook the leeks in a small quantity of boiling salted water until just tender, about 15 minutes.

Meanwhile, in another saucepan, combine the milk, carrot and onion, peppercorns, thyme, and parsley. Bring to a boil, then simmer for 5 minutes. Remove from the heat and let infuse for 10 minutes. Strain out the vegetables, bring back to a boil, and thicken with the roux to a light coating consistency. Add the mustard and two-thirds of the cheese. Season with salt and freshly ground pepper to taste.

Drain the leeks well, arrange in an oven-safe serving dish, coat with the sauce, and sprinkle with the remaining cheese mixed with a few buttered crumbs. Bake for about 15 minutes, until golden and bubbly.

# CAULIFLOWER CHEESE

Serves 6 to 8

Ah, cauliflower cheese—who doesn't love a big dish of bubbly cauliflower cheese with a layer of golden cheese melting on top? Make more than you need, reserve the cauliflower cooking water, and transform any leftovers into the most delicious soup that will have all the family begging for more. Follow the recipe below, but instead of browning in the oven or under the broiler, blend the lot with any leftover cauliflower cooking water and 3½ cups light chicken stock to make a nice consistency. Season the soup to taste and serve with croutons, cubes of diced Cheddar, and freshly chopped parsley.

1 head cauliflower with green leaves

pinch of salt

freshly chopped flat-leaf parsley, to garnish

*For the cheese sauce*

2½ cups whole milk with a dash of cream

½ onion, peeled and cut into chunks

1 small carrot, peeled and cut into chunks

6 black peppercorns

1 thyme sprig and some parsley stems

5 to 7 tablespoons Roux (page 76)

1⅓ cups shredded cheese, such as Cheddar or better still a mixture of Gruyère, Parmesan, and Cheddar

½ teaspoon Dijon mustard

sea salt and freshly ground black pepper

Preheat the oven to 425°F.

Prepare and cook the cauliflower: Remove the outer leaves and wash both the cauliflower and the leaves well. Put no more than 1 inch of water into a saucepan just large enough to fit the cauliflower; add a bit of salt. Chop the leaves into small pieces and cut the cauliflower into quarters or eighths. Place the cauliflower on top of the green leaves in the pan, cover with the lid, and simmer until cooked, 8 to 10 minutes. Test by piercing the stem with a knife—it should be tender right through.

Meanwhile, make the cheese sauce: In a saucepan, combine the milk, onion, carrot, peppercorns, and herbs. Bring to a boil, then simmer for 3 to 4 minutes. Remove from the heat and let infuse for 10 minutes.

Strain out the vegetables, return the milk to a boil, and whisk in the roux until it reaches a light coating consistency. Add most of the cheese (reserve enough to sprinkle over the dish) and the mustard. Season to taste. Spoon the sauce over the cauliflower and sprinkle with the reserved cheese. The dish may be prepared ahead to this point.

Put into the preheated oven (or under the broiler) for 3 to 4 minutes, until golden brown and bubbling. If the cauliflower cheese has cooled completely, reheat in a preheated oven at 350°F for 20 to 25 minutes. Serve sprinkled with chopped parsley.

# SUMMER FRITTATA with zucchini, basil & marjoram

Serves 2

This is one of the flat Mediterranean omelets that are simply divine for a summer lunch. Somehow one bite transports you to the magical world of Provence. It is a feast when the zucchini are fresh and crisp and no longer than 6 inches; use a mixture of green and golden. I urge you to grow a plant or two yourself even if it's only in a couple of containers in your backyard. They produce a bumper crop and you'll also have the golden flowers to use in myriad ways in salads, fritters, or even stuffed with fish or shellfish.

10 ounces crisp zucchini, not more than 6 inches in length, plus blossoms to garnish (optional)

5 tablespoons extra virgin olive oil

6 large organic, free-range eggs

2 teaspoons freshly chopped sweet marjoram or freshly torn basil leaves

4 teaspoons freshly chopped flat-leaf parsley

6 to 8 black Niçoise olives, to garnish

flaky sea salt and freshly ground black pepper

Cut the unpeeled zucchini into very thin slices. In a large sauté pan, heat 2 tablespoons of the extra virgin olive, add the zucchini, and season with salt and freshly ground pepper. Cook until al dente, 2 to 3 minutes. Drain.

In a mixing bowl, beat the eggs well and season with salt and freshly ground pepper. Add most of the herbs and finally the zucchini. In a 5 to 6-inch nonstick skillet, heat 2 tablespoons of the extra virgin olive oil over high heat and pour in the egg mixture, then reduce the heat to medium and continue to cook until the omelet is set and golden on the bottom but still juicy on top. Alternatively, using an oven-safe skillet, start by cooking on the stovetop for 3 to 4 minutes, then transfer to a preheated oven at 325°F and bake for about 10 minutes, until set.

Place a hot plate over the top of the pan and with the help of a kitchen towel quickly turn it upside down so the omelet ends up on the plate golden side upward (easier said than done!) Drizzle with the remaining olive oil and scatter a few zucchini blossoms, the black olives, and the remaining herbs over the top. Serve warm or at room temperature with a salad of organic greens and summer herbs.

# TOMATO & PESTO OMELET

Serves 1

An omelet is the ultimate fast food, but many a travesty is served up in its name. The secret is to have the pan hot enough and to use clarified butter if at all possible. Regular butter will burn if your pan is as hot as it ought to be. The omelet should be made in half the time it takes to read this recipe—your first may not be a joy to behold, but persevere, as practice makes perfect! The filling can be varied endlessly, depending on what you have on hand.

2 large organic, free-range eggs

2 teaspoons water or whole milk

2 teaspoons clarified butter (page 185)
    or olive oil

2 tablespoons Tomato Fondue (see below)

1 tablespoon wild garlic (ramps) or basil pesto

sea salt and freshly ground black pepper

*For the tomato fondue*

2 tablespoons extra virgin olive oil

scant 1 cup sliced onions

1 garlic clove, crushed

2 pounds very ripe tomatoes, sliced, or
    2 (14½-ounce) cans diced tomatoes

granulated sugar, to taste

1 tablespoon of any of the following—freshly
    chopped mint, thyme, flat-leaf parsley,
    lemon balm, and sweet marjoram or torn basil

First make the tomato fondue: In a stainless steel sauté pan or saucepan, heat the extra virgin olive oil. Add the sliced onions and garlic and toss until coated, then cover and sweat over gentle heat for until soft but not colored, about 10 minutes. Add the tomatoes with all the juice and season with sugar (canned tomatoes need lots of sugar because of their high acidity), salt, and freshly ground pepper. Add a generous sprinkling of herbs or just basil. Cover and cook until the tomato softens, 10 to 20 minutes. Then uncover and reduce slightly.

Make the omelet: Warm a plate in the oven; it must not be too hot. All your ingredients must be ready and on hand. The tomato fondue needs to be bubbling in a pot.

In a mixing bowl, using a fork, beat the eggs with the water or milk until well mixed but not too fluffy. Season with salt and pepper. Put the warm plate beside the stove. Heat a 9-inch omelet pan over high heat and add the clarified butter or olive oil. As soon as it sizzles, pour in the eggs. They will start to cook immediately, so using a metal spoon or spatula, quickly pull the edges of the omelet toward the center, tilting the pan so that the uncooked egg runs to the sides. Continue until most of the egg is set and will not run any more, a few seconds, then spoon the hot tomato fondue down the center of the omelet and drizzle the pesto over it. Immediately flip the edge just below the handle of the pan into the center to cover the filling, then hold the pan almost perpendicular over the plate so that the omelet will fold over again, then half roll, half slide the omelet onto the plate so that it lands folded in three.

# PASTA WITH FAVA BEANS, pancetta & olive oil

Fava beans are well worth growing if you have some space available. They need to be absolutely fresh, otherwise they can taste dull and mealy, as the sugars turn to starch within a few hours. So for most people it's impossible to find them freshly harvested at the peak of perfection unless you grow them or are friends with a gardener, or have a terrific farmers' market close by.

1 pound dry pasta, such as spaghetti, fettuccine, or
    tagliatelle
3 tablespoons extra virgin olive oil
4 ounces pancetta or very thin mild bacon slices,
    diced
3 garlic cloves, crushed

2¼ pounds fava beans, shelled
1 tablespoon salted butter
2 tablespoons coarsely chopped flat-leaf parsley
freshly grated Parmesan cheese, such as
    Parmigiano Reggiano or Grana Padana
sea salt

In a large pot, bring 5 quarts of water to a boil and add 1 heaping tablespoon of salt. Cook the pasta until it is almost al dente, about 5 to 8 minutes, depending on the type of pasta.

Meanwhile, in a saucepan, bring 2½ cups of water to a rolling boil, then add 1 teaspoon of salt. Add the fava beans and cook until tender, 3 to 6 minutes depending on size and freshness. Drain, refresh quickly under cold running water, and slip the beans out of their skins.

Meanwhile, in a skillet, heat most of the extra virgin olive oil, add the pancetta or bacon, and cook until crispish. Add the crushed garlic and cook for a minute or so, then add the fava beans.

When the pasta is just cooked, drain immediately and return to the pan. Toss in the butter and the remaining extra virgin olive oil, then mix with the fava bean mixture. Toss again and transfer to hot plates. Shower with the chopped parsley and grated Parmesan and serve right away.

# THE PERFECT RISOTTO

Serves 6

Risotto is one of my top ten dishes. No child should leave home without being able to whip up a gorgeous risotto, one of the easiest ways to win friends and influence people. You'll need Carnaroli, Arborio, or Vilano Nano rice. The technique is altogether different to the Indian rice pilafs, and for perfection it should be served the moment it is cooked. You can also add some dry white wine to the rice and reduce before adding the stock.

4¼ to 5½ cups homemade chicken or
    vegetable stock
6 tablespoons (¾ stick) salted butter
3 cups sliced mushrooms—porcini or cremini are
    particularly delicious
2 tablespoons extra virgin olive oil

1 onion, peeled and finely chopped
14 ounces Arborio, Carnaroli, or Vilano nano rice
½ cup freshly grated Parmesan cheese, preferably
    Parmigiano Reggiano
sea salt and freshly ground black pepper

In a saucepan, bring the stock to a boil, then reduce the heat and let simmer.

Cook the mushrooms: In another saucepan, melt 2 tablespoons of the butter. Just as it foams, add the mushrooms, season with salt and freshly ground pepper, reduce the heat, and cook long and slowly until the mushrooms are dark and concentrated in flavor. This method of cooking mushrooms transforms their flavor and makes them taste like wild mushrooms.

In a heavy-bottomed saucepan, melt another 2 tablespoons of butter with the extra virgin olive oil, add the onion, and sweat over gentle heat until soft but not colored, 4 to 5 minutes. Add the rice and stir until well coated (so far the technique is the same as for a rice pilaf and this is where people become confused). Cook for a minute or so and then add a ladleful of the simmering stock, stir continuously, and as soon as the liquid is absorbed, add another ladleful of stock. Continue to cook, stirring continuously. The heat should be brisk, but if it's too hot, the rice will be soft outside but still chewy inside, and if it's too slow, the rice will be gluey. It's difficult to know which is worse, so the trick is to regulate the heat so the rice bubbles continuously. The risotto should take about 25 to 30 minutes to cook. When it has been cooking for 20 minutes, add the cooked mushrooms and from there on add the stock about half a ladle at a time.

The risotto is done when the rice is cooked but is still ever so slightly al dente. It should be soft and creamy and quite loose rather than thick. The moment you are happy with the texture, stir in the remaining butter and the Parmesan, then taste and add more salt if necessary. Serve right away. Risotto should not hang around, otherwise it will become thick and gloopy.

# LEEK, POTATO & CHEDDAR CHEESE PIE

Serves 8

Homey and comforting, this is a super-delicious fall or winter supper dish. It also makes a delicious gratin to serve with a fine roast or a steak.

1 pound unpeeled potatoes, such as russet or
    Idaho
1 pound leeks
4 tablespoons salted butter
2½ cups Cheese Sauce (page 124), made with
    all Cheddar

½ garlic clove, crushed
2 tablespoons shredded Cheddar cheese
Buttered Crumbs (optional—page 96)
sea salt and freshly ground black pepper

Preheat the oven to 350°F.

In a saucepan, cook the potatoes in boiling salted water until tender.

Meanwhile, trim the green parts off the leeks (reserve for making stock). Wash the white parts well and cut into slices ½ inch thick. In a heavy-bottom saucepan, melt the butter and toss in the leeks. Season with salt and freshly ground pepper, cover, and cook for 5 to 6 minutes over very low heat. Turn off the heat and let them continue to cook in the covered pot in the residual heat while you make the cheese sauce, to which you add the crushed garlic; it should be a light coating consistency.

When the potatoes are cooked, drain and let cool slightly. When cool enough to handle, peel off the skins and cut into ½-inch cubes. Mix gently with the leeks and cheese sauce. Turn into a 1-quart pie dish. Sprinkle with the cheese or a mixture of the buttered crumbs and the cheese.

Bake for about 20 minutes, until golden and bubbly on top.

# TAGLIATELLE WITH CREAM & ASPARAGUS

Serves 4

We grow an old variety of green asparagus called Martha Washington—it's heaven… This dish is wickedly rich, but utterly delicious enjoyed during the spring when fresh asparagus is in season.

8 ounces asparagus

8 ounces tagliatelle, preferably fresh
   and homemade

2 tablespoons salted butter

¾ cup best-quality heavy cream

½ cup freshly grated Parmesan cheese
   (Parmigiano Reggiano is best)

freshly grated nutmeg

sea salt and freshly ground black pepper

Snap off the root end of the asparagus where it breaks naturally. In a saucepan, cook the asparagus in boiling salted water until al dente, 3 to 4 minutes. Drain and refresh in cold water, then drain again and set aside.

In a large pot, bring 4 quarts of water to a good rolling boil and add 2 tablespoons of salt. Drop in the tagliatelle and cover the pan just for a few seconds until the water comes back to a boil. Cook the tagliatelle until barely al dente (remember it will cook a bit more with the sauce). Homemade tagliatelle will take only 1 to 2 minutes; dry pasta will take considerably longer, 10 to 12 minutes depending on the brand. Drain the pasta and reserve some of the pasta cooking water in case the sauce needs to be loosened.

Cut the asparagus into thin slices, no thicker than ¼ inch, on the bias. In a wide saucepan, melt the butter, add half the cream, and simmer just until the cream thickens slightly, about 2 minutes. Add the asparagus, the drained tagliatelle, remaining cream, and the Parmesan. Season with a small amount of grated nutmeg, sea salt, and freshly ground pepper. Toss briefly just enough to coat the pasta and check the seasoning. Serve right away.

# PROVENÇALE BEAN STEW

Serves 6 to 8

This is a delicious rustic bean stew, inexpensive to make yet wonderfully filling and nutritious, and a particularly good dish for vegetarians. Do not add the salt to the beans until near the end of the cooking time, otherwise they tend to harden. Add some Aleppo pepper or a few red pepper flakes if desired, and of course you can add some spicy merguez sausages or chorizo if you wish. If this bean stew is being eaten without meat, rice should be eaten in the same meal to ensure maximum nutritional benefit from the beans.

scant ⅔ cup dry navy beans

scant ⅔ cup dry red kidney beans

⅔ cup dry black-eyed peas

3 small carrots, peeled

3 onions, peeled

4 bouquet garni made up of sweet marjoram
   and flat-leaf parsley

2 tablespoons extra virgin olive oil

2 cups sliced onions

1 large red bell pepper, cored, seeded, and sliced

1 large green bell pepper, cored, seeded, and sliced

2 garlic cloves, crushed

1 (14½-oz) can diced tomatoes or 1 pound peeled
   very ripe fresh tomatoes, chopped

2 tablespoons Tomato Puree (page 18)

1 tablespoon freshly chopped sweet marjoram,
   thyme, or basil

pinch of granulated sugar

⅓ cup black Kalamata olives

2 tablespoons freshly chopped flat-leaf parsley or
   cilantro, plus more to garnish

sea salt and freshly ground black pepper and sugar

Soak the two different types of beans and black-eyed peas separately in plenty of cold water overnight. Next day, drain, put into three separate saucepans, and cover with fresh cold water. Add a carrot, an onion, and a bouquet garni to each pan. Bring to a boil and boil rapidly for 10 minutes, then cover and simmer until tender but not mushy. Dried beans and peas take anything from 20 minutes to 1 hour to cook, depending on their variety and age, so it is better to cook them separately and combine them later. Add a pinch of salt toward the end of cooking.

When the beans and peas are cooked, drain and reserve 1¼ cups of the cooking liquid, discarding the vegetables and bouquet garni. In a heavy-bottom pan, heat the olive oil and sweat the sliced onions over low heat until sweet and slightly golden, about 5 minutes. Add the bell peppers and garlic, cover, and continue to sweat gently for 10 minutes. Add the tomatoes with their juice, tomato puree, marjoram, thyme, or basil, the cooked beans and peas, remaining bouquet garni, reserved bean cooking liquid, salt, freshly ground pepper, and sugar. Cover and simmer until the bell peppers are cooked, about 20 minutes. Five minutes before the end of the cooking time, add the olives and freshly chopped parsley or cilantro. Remove the bouquet garni and season to taste. Serve garnished with more chopped parsley or cilantro.

# POTATO, CARROT & CAULIFLOWER CURRY
## with cilantro & toasted almonds

Serves 4

Sophie Grigson, the bubbly cook of the many earrings, made this exceptionally delicious vegetable curry when she was guest chef at the school in 1993 and we've been enjoying it ever since.

7 ounces unpeeled small new potatoes
   or other waxy potatoes

7 ounces cauliflower florets

7 ounces carrots, peeled and sliced on the bias

4 green cardamon pods

1 tablespoon coriander seeds

2 teaspoons cumin seeds

2 dried red chilies, seeded and broken into pieces

¼ cup unsweetened shredded coconut

1 scant teaspoon grated fresh ginger

1 cup thick plain yogurt or labneh

3 tablespoons salted butter

2 tablespoons extra virgin olive oil

1 small onion, peeled and grated

2 tablespoons water

¼ cup toasted sliced almonds, to garnish

1 tablespoon freshly chopped cilantro leaves
   to garnish

In a saucepan, cook the potatoes in boiling salted water until just tender. Drain and let cool slightly. When cool enough to handle, peel off the skins and halve or quarter depending on size. Steam or boil the cauliflower until barely cooked, then drain well. Steam or boil the carrots until just cooked, then drain well.

Split the cardamon pods and extract the seeds. Mix with the coriander and cumin seeds. In a heavy skillet, dry-roast the seeds over high heat until they smell aromatic. Transfer to a bowl. Dry-roast the chilies (which makes them easier to grind), add the coconut, and cook until pale golden, then mix with the spices. Let cool. Using a spice grinder or food processor, blitz to a powder. Combine the spice mix with the ginger and yogurt.

In a sauté pan or skillet, melt the butter with the oil. Cook the potatoes, cauliflower, and carrots briskly until patched with brown. Remove with a slotted spoon and set aside. Add the onion to the fat and cook until golden brown, then stir in the thick yogurt mixture a tablespoon at a time. Cook, stirring, for 2 minutes, then stir in the water, followed by the potatoes and cauliflower. Stir until piping hot. Serve sprinkled with the toasted almonds and cilantro leaves.

# BAKED EGGS WITH MANY GOOD THINGS

Serves 4

Great as an appetizer or a snack, there are infinite variations on this theme, but the eggs must be super fresh and the cream rich.

1 tablespoon salted butter
6 to 8 tablespoons rich heavy cream
4 large very fresh organic, free-range eggs
flaky sea salt and freshly ground black pepper

Lightly grease four small ramekins with the butter. In a saucepan, heat the cream. When it is hot, spoon about 1 tablespoon into each ramekin and break an egg into the cream. Season with flaky sea salt and freshly ground pepper. Spoon the remaining cream over the top of the eggs. Place the ramekins in a bain-marie—a wide pan filled with enough hot water to come halfway up the sides of the ramekins. Cover with aluminum foil or a lid and bring to simmering point on the stovetop. Continue to cook gently for about 10 minutes for a soft-cooked egg, 12 minutes for a medium-cooked egg. Serve right away.

## VARIATIONS

⌐ *Baked Eggs with Cheese* Sprinkle ½ to 1 tablespoon of grated Parmesan, Gruyère, or Cheddar cheese or a mixture of all three on top of each egg. Bake, uncovered, in a bain-marie in the oven if you prefer.

⌐ *Baked Eggs with Tomato Fondue* Add 1 tablespoon of Tomato Fondue (page 127) to each ramekin instead of the cream before adding the egg. Proceed as in the master recipe, with or without the cheese.

⌐ *Baked Eggs with Smoked Salmon or Mackerel* Put 1 tablespoon of chopped smoked salmon or flaked smoked mackerel in the bottom of each ramekin. Add 1 to 2 tablespoons of freshly chopped flat-leaf parsley to the cream and proceed as in the master recipe.

⌐ *Baked Eggs with Fresh Herbs & Dijon Mustard* Use 3 tablespoons in total of flat-leaf parsley, tarragon, chives, and chervil. Mix 2 teaspoons of Dijon mustard and 3 tablespoons of freshly chopped herbs into the cream and proceed as for the master recipe.

⌐ *Baked Eggs with Yogurt & Paprika Oil* Place a spoonful of plain yogurt on top just before serving. Drizzle with paprika oil—just gently heat 1 teaspoon of sweet or smoked paprika in ¼ cup extra virgin olive oil.

# LEEKS WITH YELLOW BELL PEPPERS & HERBS

Serves 6

I love to roast or chargrill leeks, but this braised version is also irresistible served as a side dish or light lunch in crisp pastry tartlets or in phyllo triangles as an appetizer.

6 young leeks, about 1 inch in diameter
3 yellow bell peppers
1 tablespoon salted butter
1 tablespoon extra virgin olive oil

1 to 2 tablespoons freshly chopped sweet
    marjoram or a mixture of parsley, basil, and
    marjoram
sea salt and freshly ground black pepper

Wash and slice the leeks into slices ¼ inch thick. Quarter the bell peppers, core, and seed, then cut into slices ¼ inch thick on the bias. In a heavy-bottom saucepan, melt the butter with the extra virgin oil and toss in the leeks. Season with salt and freshly ground pepper. Cover and sweat over gentle heat until tender, about 8 minutes. Add the bell peppers, toss, and add a drop of water if necessary. Add half the herbs, cover, and continue to cook until the peppers are soft. Add the remaining herbs, season to taste, and serve.

## VARIATION

*Leek, Yellow Bell Pepper & Marjoram Tart* Fill a fully baked savory tart shell with the cooked vegetable mixture and serve right away. Alternatively, prebake tartlet shells. Beat ¾ cup light cream with 2 large organic, free-range egg yolks, then combine with the leek and bell pepper mixture, season, and fill the tartlets. Bake in a preheated oven at 350°F for about 15 minutes.

# salads

# ROAST RED BELL PEPPER & LENTIL SALAD
with soft goat cheese

Serves 6

The sweetness of the red bell peppers complements the goat cheese and lentils perfectly. A few slices of warm duck breast would be a delicious instead of the goat cheese here.

1 cup plus 2 tablespoons dry Puy or Castelluccio lentils

1 carrot, peeled

1 onion, peeled and stuck with 2 cloves

1 bouquet garni

extra virgin olive oil

large handful of finely chopped fresh herbs, such as sweet marjoram or flat-leaf parsley

freshly squeezed lemon juice

4 red bell peppers, freshly roasted, peeled, seeded, and chopped

soft goat cheese, preferably Irish St. Tola or Ardsallagh, sliced

sea salt and freshly ground black pepper

arugula leaves and lemon wedges, to garnish

Wash and drain the lentils, put them into a saucepan, and cover with fresh cold water. Add the carrot, onion, and bouquet garni and bring slowly to a boil. Reduce the heat and simmer very gently for 10 to 15 minutes, testing for doneness regularly. The lentils should be al dente but not hard. Strain and discard the carrot, onion, and bouquet garni. Season the lentils while still warm with some extra virgin olive oil, then add some of the herbs and lots of freshly squeezed lemon juice. Season to taste with sea salt and freshly ground pepper.

Arrange the still-warm lentils on a plate or plates and top with the freshly roasted red bell pepper and some slices of goat cheese. Garnish with a few arugula leaves and a couple of lemon wedges. Sprinkle with the remaining chopped herbs and serve warm.

# APPLE, CELERY & WALNUT SALAD
with spicy chicken

Serves 6

A little twist on the famous Waldorf Salad; the spicy chicken perks up the original, but of course can be omitted if you would prefer the classic combination.

½ head celery, cut into 1½-inch lengths

8 ounces green apples, such as Granny Smith

8 ounces red apples, such as Gala

2 tablespoons freshly squeezed
   lemon juice, or to taste

1 teaspoon granulated sugar, or to taste

⅔ cup Homemade Mayonnaise (page 146)

½ cup fresh walnut halves, coarsely chopped

freshly chopped flat-leaf parsley

1 head crisp lettuce, leaves separated

watercress sprigs

For the spicy chicken

1 tablespoon ground cumin

1 tablespoon sweet paprika

1 to 1½ teaspoons cayenne pepper

1 tablespoon ground turmeric

1 teaspoon granulated sugar

1 teaspoon freshly ground black pepper

2 teaspoons sea salt

3 garlic cloves, crushed

5 tablespoons freshly squeezed lemon juice

2 organic, free-range chicken breast halves

2 to 3 tablespoons sunflower oil

Make the spicy chicken: In a bowl, combine the cumin, paprika, cayenne, turmeric, sugar, black pepper, salt, garlic, and lemon juice. Using a sharp knife, slash the chicken in a couple of places. Rub the spice paste all over the chicken, put in a bowl, and cover with plastic wrap. Let marinate in the refrigerator for at least 3 hours.

Preheat the oven to 350°F. Put the chicken into a roasting pan with all the paste. Brush or drizzle with the sunflower oil and bake for about 20 minutes, then turn over and bake for another 20 to 25 minutes, depending on the size of the chicken pieces, until cooked through. Baste 2 or 3 times during cooking. Transfer to a serving dish, spoon the degreased drippings, over the chicken, and let cool.

Soak the celery in a bowl of ice water for 15 to 30 minutes. Core the apples and cut into ½-inch dice. In a bowl, combine most of the freshly squeezed lemon juice and sugar (reserve a bit of both) and 1 tablespoon of the mayonnaise. Toss the diced apple in the dressing and set aside while you prepare the remaining ingredients.

Drain the celery and add to the apple with most of the walnuts, the remaining mayonnaise, and some chopped parsley, and mix thoroughly. Taste and add more lemon juice or sugar if necessary. Slice the cold spiced chicken crosswise and toss lightly through the salad.

Place a few crisp lettuce leaves on each plate and pile the salad alongside. Add a few watercress sprigs, scatter the remaining walnuts on top, and sprinkle with chopped parsley.

# POTATO & SCALLION SALAD

Serves 4 to 6

Everyone insists that potato salad ought to be made with waxy potatoes, but I prefer floury potatoes for superb flavor. Potato salad may be used as a base for other salads and can be bulked out with the addition of cubes of fennel bulb, salami, cooked kabanossi sausage, or, most delicious of all, cooked mussels.

2¼ pounds freshly cooked potatoes, diced

⅓ cup plus 2 tablespoons Ballymaloe French Dressing (page 147)

2 tablespoons freshly chopped scallions or chives

2 tablespoons freshly chopped flat-leaf parsley

⅓ cup plus 2 tablespoons Homemade Mayonnaise (see right)

flaky sea salt and freshly ground black pepper

*For the homemade mayonnaise*

2 large organic, free-range egg yolks (reserve the whites for making meringue)

pinch of English mustard powder or ¼ teaspoon French mustard

½ teaspoon salt

2 teaspoons white wine vinegar

1 cup sunflower or olive oil or a mixture – I use ¾ cup sunflower oil and ¼ cup olive oil

freshly ground black pepper

Make the mayonnaise: Put the egg yolks into a Pyrex bowl with the mustard, salt, and white wine vinegar. Put the oil into a measuring cup with a good pouring spout. Take a wire whisk in one hand and the oil in the other and drip the oil onto the egg yolks, drop by drop, whisking continuously. Within a minute you will notice that the mixture is beginning to thicken. When this happens you can add the oil a bit faster, but do not get too cheeky or it will suddenly curdle because the egg yolks can only absorb the oil at a certain pace. Taste and add more seasoning if necessary.

If the mayonnaise curdles it will suddenly become quite thin, and if left sitting the oil will start to float to the top of the sauce. If this happens, you can quite easily rectify the situation by putting another egg yolk or 1 to 2 tablespoons of boiling water into a clean bowl, then whisk in the curdled mayonnaise, ½ teaspoon at a time, until it re-emulsifies.

The potatoes will have maximum flavor if they are boiled in their skins and peeled, diced, and measured while still warm.

In a bowl, coat the diced potatoes with the Ballymaloe French dressing and immediately combine with the scallions or chives and parsley. Season well with flaky sea salt and freshly ground pepper. Let cool and finally add the mayonnaise. This salad keeps well in the refrigerator for about 2 days.

# PUY LENTIL, BEAN & whatever you fancy salad

Serves 6

This salad is delicious on its own but can be used as a vehicle to use up loads of other ingredients in your fridge or pantry—try adding tuna, flaked salmon or smoked mackerel, bell peppers, chorizo, or warm crispy bacon.

¼ cup dry navy beans

¼ cup dry red kidney beans

¼ cup dry Puy lentils

3 small carrots, peeled

3 small onions, peeled and each stuck with 2 cloves

3 bouquet garni

2 teaspoons freshly chopped parsley

2 teaspoons freshly chopped basil

*For the Ballymaloe French dressing*

1 shallot, peeled and finely chopped

1 cup extra virgin olive oil

3 tablespoons red or white wine vinegar

2 teaspoons Dijon mustard

1 teaspoon finely chopped chives

3 large garlic cloves, crushed

1 teaspoon finely chopped thyme

1 teaspoon finely chopped flat-leaf parsley

sea salt and freshly ground black pepper

Soak the two different types of beans separately in plenty of cold water overnight. Next day, drain and put into two separate saucepans, and put the lentils into a third saucepan. Cover with fresh cold water. Add a carrot, an onion, and a bouquet garni to each pan. Bring to a boil and boil rapidly for 10 minutes, then cover and simmer until soft but still holding their shape. Dried beans take anything from 20 minutes to 1 hour to cook, depending on their variety and age; lentils 15 to 20 minutes. Add a pinch of salt toward the end of cooking.

Meanwhile, make the French dressing: In a bowl or using a blender, beat or blend together all the ingredients. The dressing should be very well seasoned and quite sharp.

When the beans and lentils are cooked, drain them well. (Reserve the cooking liquids—use as a base for a bean or lentil soup, as they are full of vitamins and protein.) While they are still warm, toss the beans and lentils in the French dressing, using enough just to coat them. Season to taste with salt and freshly ground pepper, and fold in the chopped parsley and basil.

# A WARM SALAD WITH IRISH BLUE CHEESE

Serves 4

Some ripe, crumbly Cashel Blue cheese, now made by Jane and Louis Grubb's daughter Sarah, would be wonderful for this salad. We also love their Crozier Blue cheese. A few small cubes of ripe pear are delicious here too.

selection of organic salad greens, such as
    watercress, radicchio, Belgian endive, arugula,
    oak leaf, and butterhead
12 slices thin sourdough baguette, ¼ inch thick
3 tablespoons salted butter, softened
1 garlic clove, peeled
5 ounces smoked bacon, cut into ¼-inch lardons
extra virgin olive oil, for cooking
2 ounces blue cheese, preferably Irish Cashel Blue
    or Crozier Blue
1 heaping tablespoon chervil sprigs or freshly
    chopped flat-leaf parsley

*For the vinaigrette dressing*
1 tablespoon balsamic vinegar
3 tablespoons extra virgin olive oil
2 teaspoons freshly chopped chervil and
    2 teaspoons freshly chopped tarragon, or
    4 teaspoons freshly chopped flat-leaf parsley
sea salt and freshly ground black pepper

Preheat the oven to 350°F.

Make the vinaigrette dressing: In a small bowl, beat together all the ingredients.

Wash and dry the salad greens, then tear into bite-size pieces and put into a salad bowl. Spread both sides of the bread slices with the softened butter. Place on a baking sheet and bake for about 20 minutes, until golden and crisp on both sides. Rub with the garlic clove and keep hot in the oven on low with the door slightly open.

In a saucepan, blanch the bacon in boiling water, then drain and refresh in cold water. Dry well on paper towels. Just before serving, in a skillet, sauté the lardons in a splash of extra virgin olive oil until golden.

To serve, dress the salad greens with just enough of the vinaigrette to make them glisten. Crumble the cheese with a fork and add it to the salad, tossing well together. Divide among four plates. Scatter the hot crispy bacon over the top, place three warm croutons on each plate, and sprinkle the chervil sprigs or chopped parsley over the salad. Alternatively, arrange the salad on a large serving plate with the croutons around the edge. Serve right away with the remaining vinaigrette in a small bowl.

# RED & YELLOW TOMATO SALAD
with mint or basil

Serves 8

A perfect tomato salad is a wonderful thing. In the late summer when we have intensively sweet vine-ripened tomatoes we often serve a tomato salad as a first course. The flavor is so sublime, it is a revelation to many people who have forgotten what a tomato should taste like. Tomato salad complements so many other dishes—add some torn fresh mozzarella or burrata and a few basil leaves for a Salad Caprese. A simple tomato salad is great with savory tarts or quiche or some poached or warm smoked salmon.

8 to 12 very ripe firm tomatoes
pinch of granulated sugar
2 to 3 tablespoons Ballymaloe French Dressing
  (page 147)

2 to 4 teaspoons torn fresh basil leaves or freshly
  chopped mint
sea salt and freshly ground black pepper

Using the point of a vegetable knife, remove the core from each tomato. Cut some tomatoes around the equator into 3 or 4 slices and others into quarters or random shapes. Arrange in a single layer on a flat plate, then sprinkle with the sugar, salt, and several grinds of black pepper. Toss immediately in just enough Ballymaloe French dressing to coat the tomatoes, pile them onto a serving plate, and sprinkle with the torn basil or chopped mint. Tomatoes must be dressed as soon as they are cut to seal in their flavor.

## VARIATION

*Heirloom Tomato Salad*  Use a mixture of vine-ripened heirloom tomatoes in the recipe above and instead of Ballymaloe French dressing I love to use freshly squeezed lemon juice, with best-quality extra virgin olive oil and a drizzle of honey.

# A WARM SALAD OF IRISH GOAT CHEESE
## with walnut oil dressing

Serves 4

This is a perfect supper dish; include a few cherry tomatoes or strips of roasted red bell pepper if you want to make it more substantial. It can also be served as an appetizer or as a cheese course. Walnuts and walnut oil must be fresh, as they go rancid and bitter quite quickly, so store in a cool place.

selection of lettuces and salad greens, such as
    butterhead, frisée, oak leaf, radicchio
    trevisano, arugula, salad burnet, and
    golden marjoram
12 slices small baguette, 3 inches thick, toasted
1 fresh soft goat cheese, preferably Irish
    Ardsailagh, St. Tola, or Lough Caum
drizzle of honey

16 to 20 fresh walnut halves
chive or wild garlic (ramps) flowers or marigold
    petals (*Calendula officinalis*) in season,
    to garnish

*For the walnut oil dressing*
6 tablespoons walnut oil or extra virgin olive oil
2 tablespoons white wine vinegar
dash of Dijon mustard

Wash and dry the salad greens, then tear the larger leaves into bite-size pieces.

Make the walnut oil dressing: In a small bowl, beat together all the ingredients. Cover each piece of toasted French bread with a slice of goat cheese ¾ inch thick. Just before serving, preheat the broiler. Broil the cheese-topped bread until the cheese is soft and slightly golden, 5 to 6 minutes.

Meanwhile, in a bowl, toss the salad greens lightly in just enough dressing to make them glisten, then drop a small handful onto each plate. Place three hot goat cheese croutons on each salad, drizzle with honey, and scatter with a few walnut pieces. I sprinkle chive or wild garlic (ramps) flowers or marigold petals over the salad in season. Serve right away.

# A WARM WINTER SALAD WITH DUCK LIVERS
## & hazelnut oil dressing

Serves 4

I love this combination of warm livers and perfumed leaves. I am an organ meats fiend, but pretty fussy about sourcing organic.

selection of salad greens, such as butterhead, radicchio, trevisano, and oak leaf

6 fresh organic duck or chicken livers

4 ounces carrots

4 ounces celery root (celeriac)

1 tablespoon salted butter

12 Belgian endive leaves

watercress sprigs

sea salt and freshly ground black pepper

1 tablespoon freshly chopped chives, to garnish

*For the hazelnut oil dressing*

6 tablespoons fresh hazelnut oil

2 tablespoons white wine vinegar (I love Forum Chardonnay vinegar)

Wash and dry the salad greens, then tear them into bite-size pieces. Wash the livers and divide each lobe into two pieces. Dry on paper towels and keep refrigerated.

Make the hazelnut oil dressing: In a small bowl, beat together the ingredients. Peel the carrot and celery root, then shred on the large part of a grater. In a bowl, toss in about 3 tablespoons of the dressing. Season to taste. In another bowl, toss the salad greens in just enough of the dressing to make them glisten.

In a sauté pan, melt the butter; season the livers and cook over gentle heat for a minute or two, tossing frequently. While the livers are cooking, arrange three endive leaves in a star shape on each plate. Place a mound of salad greens in the center, tuck in a few watercress sprigs, and top with some shredded carrot and celery root. Finally, while still warm, arrange three pieces of liver on each salad. Sprinkle with the finely chopped chives to garnish.

# BEANS GALORE with toasted hazelnuts & cilantro

Serves 8

Dried beans and legumes are a brilliant and inexpensive source of protein, particularly important for vegetarians and vegans. In this salad we combine them with freshly cooked green beans. The secret of a super salad is to toss the beans in a well-flavored dressing while they are still warm. Each has its own particular flavor, so experiment with different combinations. Chickpeas (garbanzo beans) are also excellent, and a tahini dressing drizzled over the salad adds a totally different dimension that I love.

scant ⅔ cup dry navy beans

scant ⅔ cup dry red kidney beans

scant ⅔ cup dry flageolet beans

⅔ cup dry black-eyed peas

4 small carrots, peeled

4 small onions, peeled

4 bouquet garni

3 teaspoons salt

1 pound green beans

1¼ cup Ballymaloe French Dressing (page 147)

2 tablespoons freshly chopped flat-leaf parsley

2 tablespoons freshly chopped cilantro,
    plus sprigs to garnish

freshly squeezed lemon juice (optional)

¾ cup toasted hazelnuts, halved

sea salt and freshly ground black pepper

lemon wedges, to garnish

Soak the three different types of beans and black-eyed peas separately in plenty of cold water overnight. Next day, drain, put into four separate saucepans, and cover with fresh cold water. Add a carrot, an onion, and a bouquet garni to each pan. Bring to a boil and boil rapidly for 10 minutes, then cover and simmer until just tender. Dried beans and peas take anything from 20 minutes to 1 hour to cook, depending on their variety and age. Drain well. (Reserve the cooking liquid for soup.)

In a saucepan, bring 1 quart of water to a fast rolling boil, add the salt, and toss in the green beans. Boil very fast until just cooked, retaining a bit of bite, 5 to 6 minutes. Drain immediately.

In a salad bowl, while still warm, toss all the beans and peas in the French dressing. Add the chopped parsley and cilantro, and season well with sea salt and freshly ground pepper. Taste and sharpen with freshly squeezed lemon juice if it doesn't seem perky enough. Scatter with the toasted hazelnuts and cilantro sprigs, and garnish with lemon wedges.

## VARIATION

*Tahini Sauce* Use this sauce, from my brother Rory O'Connell, instead of the French dressing. In a blender, blend ½ cup tahini, 1 crushed garlic clove, pinch of salt, juice of ½ organic lemon, and ¼ cup water to a creamy, slightly thick pouring consistency, adding more water, lemon juice, and salt as necessary for the correct consistency, acidity level, and seasoning.

# TRADITIONAL GREEK SALAD
with marinated feta or bocconcini

Serves 6

This salad is served in virtually every taverna in Greece and is delicious when made with really fresh ingredients and eaten immediately. We now make our own feta cheese in our micro dairy, or use Toonsbridge or Ardsallagh feta or our local Knockalara ewe milk cheese instead of feta, which is seldom in the condition that the Greeks intended by the time it reaches us! I also use Mani olive oil made from the Kóroneiki olive. You can serve this salad in a pita bread—just split it in half across or lengthwise and fill with the drained Greek salad and shredded lettuce.

3 ounces feta or whole bocconcini (cut the bocconcini in half if very large)

5 tablespoons extra virgin olive oil

3 tablespoons freshly chopped sweet marjoram

½ to 1 crisp cucumber

1 to 2 red onions or 6 scallions

6 very ripe tomatoes

12 to 18 Kalamata olives

1 tablespoon freshly squeezed lemon juice

granulated sugar, to taste

sea salt and freshly ground black pepper

freshly chopped flat-leaf parsley, to garnish

If using feta, cut it into 1-inch cubes. Drizzle with 2 tablespoons of the extra virgin olive oil and 1 tablespoon of the chopped marjoram.

Just before serving, halve the cucumber lengthwise and cut into chunks. Peel and slice the red onions or coarsely chop the green and white parts of the scallions. Core the tomatoes and cut into wedges. In a salad bowl, combine the tomatoes, cucumber, onions, olives, and remaining chopped marjoram.

Drizzle with the remaining extra virgin olive oil and the freshly squeezed lemon juice. Season to taste with sugar, salt, and freshly ground pepper, and toss well. Sprinkle with the feta cubes or add the bocconcini, and garnish with chopped flat-leaf parsley. Do not toss. Serve right away, otherwise it will become watery and tired.

# SUMMER GREEN SALAD
with honey & mustard dressing

Serves 4

At Ballymaloe we serve a salad of organic greens all year round at every lunch and dinner. It varies throughout the seasons depending on what's in the gardens and greenhouse and what wild greens and edible flowers we have access to.

1 head mild lettuce, such as butterhead
selection of the following—finely chopped flat-leaf parsley, mint, or any herbs of your fancy, scallions, diced cucumber, garden cress, watercress, pea shoots, fava bean tops, romaine, radicchio, oak leaf, Chinese cabbage, arugula, salad burnet, and any other interesting lettuces available

*For the honey & mustard dressing*
⅔ cup olive oil or a mixture of olive and other oils, such as sunflower and peanut
3½ tablespoons white wine vinegar
2 teaspoons honey
2 heaped teaspoons whole grain mustard
2 garlic cloves, crushed
sea salt and freshly ground black pepper

Make the honey and mustard dressing: In a small bowl, beat together all the ingredients and beat well again before use.

Wash and dry the lettuces and other greens very carefully. Tear into bite-size pieces and put into a deep salad bowl with the other chosen ingredients. Cover with plastic wrap and refrigerate if not to be served immediately.

Just before serving, toss the salad greens with just enough dressing to make them glisten. The salad must not be dressed until just before serving, otherwise it will be tired and unappetizing. Serve right away.

## VARIATIONS

⌐ *Summer Green Salad with Edible Flowers*  Prepare a selection of salad greens (see above) and add some edible flowers, such as marigold petals, nasturtium flowers, borage flowers, chive flowers, or arugula blossoms—one or all of these or some other herb flowers could be added. Toss with a well-flavored dressing just before serving. This salad could be served as a basis for an appetizer salad or as an accompanying salad to a main course. Remember to use restraint with the flowers!

⌐ *Farmers' Market Salad with Aged Coolea & Pomegranate Seeds*  Sprinkle some pomegranate seeds and shavings of aged Coolea cheese over the salad (follow the recipe as above). You can vary the dressings—some pomegranate molasses would be particularly good.

# CARROT & APPLE SALAD
## with honey & vinegar dressing

Serves 6

This gorgeous salad can be made in minutes from ingredients you would probably have easily on hand, but should not be prepared more than 30 minutes ahead, as the apple will discolor. Serve either as an appetizer or as an accompanying salad with glazed ham or pork with crackling (page 78). Choose best-quality wine vinegar and pure unadulterated honey.

2 cups shredded carrot
2½ cups shredded apple, such as Braeburn
a few small lettuce leaves
sea salt and freshly ground black pepper
watercress or flat-leaf parsley sprigs and wild
    garlic (ramps) or chive flowers in season,
    to garnish

*For the honey & vinegar dressing*
2 generous teaspoons honey
1 tablespoon white wine vinegar (I use Forum
    Chardonnay vinegar)

Make the honey and vinegar dressing: In a small bowl, dissolve the honey in the wine vinegar.

In a large bowl, combine the shredded carrot and apple, add the dressing, and toss to coat. Taste and add a bit more honey or vinegar, depending on the sweetness of the apple.

Take six large side plates; white are best for this. Arrange a few small lettuce leaves on each plate and add the dressed carrot and apple.

Garnish with watercress or parsley sprigs and sprinkle with wild garlic (ramps) or chive flowers in season. Season to taste.

# KINOITH GARDEN SALAD

Serves 4

Visitors to Ireland complain over and over again that it is virtually impossible to get a green salad in a restaurant. It does in fact appear on menus regularly, but when it is served it often includes tomato, cucumber, bell pepper, and sometimes even raw onion rings—not the mixture of lettuce and salad greens that people had hoped for. I think it's best to keep it simple, served with a well-seasoned dressing made with extra virgin olive oil and wine vinegar and including a few edible flowers and foraged greens if the fancy takes you.

This is a rather elaborate version that we make in summer from what is in season in the garden. A simple dressing of three parts extra virgin olive oil to one part wine vinegar, seasoned with a little salt and freshly ground pepper, makes a splendid dressing. Choose a really good extra virgin olive oil such as Capezzana, Fontodi or Selvapiana.

selection of fresh lettuces, salad greens, herbs, and edible flowers, such as butterhead, oak leaf, pea shoots, saladisi, lollo rosso, radicchio, frisée, mizuna, purslane, red orach, arugula, edible chrysanthemum leaves, wild sorrel leaves or buckler leaf sorrel, chervil, golden marjoram, salad burnet, borage, zucchini or squash blossoms, sage flowers, nasturtium flowers and tiny leaves, marigold petals, chive or wild garlic (ramps) flowers, and herb leaves, such as lemon balm, mint, flat-leaf parsley, chervil, lovage, tiny tarragon, dill weed, or sweet marjoram sprigs

*For the dressing*

¼ cup extra virgin olive oil

1 tablespoon white wine vinegar (I use Forum Chardonnay vinegar)

1 teaspoon honey

1 teaspoon whole grain mustard

1 garlic clove, crushed

flaky sea salt and freshly ground black pepper

Make the dressing: In a small bowl, beat together all the dressing ingredients. Store in a jar with a screw-on lid and shake to re-emulsify if not serving immediately.

In a large, deep salad bowl, combine your selection of lettuce, salad greens, herbs, and edible flowers. Just before serving, toss with just enough of the dressing to make the leaves glisten. Sprinkle a few more edible flowers over the top. Serve right away.

desserts

# ALMOND TARTLETS or tarts with raspberries

Serves 12/
Makes 24 tartlets
or 2 tarts

These tartlets are gems. They are also delicious with just a spoonful of raspberry jam and a dollop of cream. Try to use shallow tartlet pans, and you'll need the best-quality ground almonds you can find.

½ cup (1 stick) butter, softened

½ cup superfine sugar

1 cup plus 2 tablespoons almond flour

tiny lemon balm or rose geranium leaves
   (*Pelargonium graveolens*), to decorate

*For the red currant glaze*

heaping 1 cup red currant jelly

1 tablespoon lemon juice or water (optional)

*For the filling*

whichever ripe fruit is in season, such as
   fresh raspberries or loganberries, halved
   strawberries, red currants, black currants,
   poached rhubarb, sliced fresh peaches
   or nectarines, peeled and seeded grapes,
   or blueberries

1¼ cups whipped cream

Preheat the oven to 350°F.

In a mixing bowl, cream the butter, then mix in the sugar and almond flour but do not overbeat. Divide the mixture equally among the cavities of two 12-cavity mini tart pans or between two 7-inch round shallow cake pans and press down over the bottom and sides to make tartlet or tart shells. Bake for 20 to 30 minutes or until golden brown. The tartlet or tart shells will be too soft to turn out immediately, so let cool for about 5 minutes before removing from the pans. Do not allow to set hard or the butter will solidify and they will stick to the pans. If this happens, return the pans to the oven for a few minutes so the butter melts and then they will slide out easily. Let cool on a wire rack.

Make the red currant glaze: In a small stainless steel saucepan, melt the red currant jelly and add the liquid to thin if necessary. Stir gently, but do not beat or it will become cloudy. Cook for just 1 to 2 minutes or the jelly will darken. Store any leftover glaze in an airtight jar and reheat gently to melt before use. The quantities given above make a generous 1¼ cups of glaze.

Just before serving, arrange the raspberries, loganberries, or other selection of fruit in the tartlet or tart shells. Brush with the red currant jelly glaze. Top with piped rosettes of whipped cream and decorate with tiny lemon balm or rose geranium leaves.

# ORANGE MOUSSE with dark chocolate wafers

Serves 6 to 8

This mousse sounds slightly retro now, but everyone loves it when we serve it on the sweet trolley at Ballymaloe House. Be careful to measure the gelatin accurately.

2 oranges (1½ if very large)

4 large organic, free-range eggs, 2 separated

⅓ cup superfine sugar

3 tablespoons water

2 teaspoons gelatin powder

1 organic lemon

1 cup softly whipped cream

*For the chocolate wafers*

2 ounces best-quality semisweet chocolate

*To decorate*

2 oranges

1 cup whipped cream

pinch of superfine sugar, or to taste

Wash and dry the oranges. Using the finest part of a stainless steel grater, grate the orange zest. Put into a mixing bowl with the two whole eggs, two egg yolks, and the superfine sugar. Using a handheld electric mixer, whisk to a thick mousse. Put the water into a small heat-safe bowl, measure the gelatin carefully, and sprinkle it over the water. Let soak for a few minutes until the gelatin has absorbed the water and feels spongy to the touch. Sit the bowl in a saucepan of simmering water and let the gelatin dissolve completely—all the granules will dissolve and it should look perfectly clear.

Meanwhile, squeeze the juice from the oranges and the lemon, measure, and if necessary bring up to 1¼ cups with more orange juice. Stir a bit into the gelatin, then mix the gelatine mixture well with the remaining juice. Gently stir into the mousse. Let cool in the refrigerator, stirring regularly, until the mousse is just beginning to set around the edges, then fold in the softly whipped cream. In a mixing bowl, whisk the two egg whites until stiff, then gently fold into the mousse. Pour into a glass bowl or individual glasses. Cover and let set in the refrigerator for 3 to 4 hours or, better still, overnight.

Meanwhile, make the chocolate wafers: In a heat-safe bowl set over a saucepan of barely simmering water, melt the chocolate, stirring until smooth. Spread onto a nonstick baking mat or heavy baking sheet. Let set in a cool place until firm enough to cut into squares or diamonds.

While the chocolate is setting, make the orange-flavored cream: Grate the peel of one orange, then combine half with the whipped cream and superfine sugar to taste. Peel and section both oranges. Decorate the top of the mousse with the orange sections and pipe on some rosettes of orange-flavored cream. Sprinkle with the grated orange zest. Peel the chocolate wafers off the mat or baking sheet and use them to decorate the edges of the mousse.

# CARAMEL MOUSSE WITH PRALINE

Serves 6

*A light and rich mousse; caramel and praline make a very special combination of flavors.*

1 cup plus 2 tablespoons granulated sugar

4 large organic, free-range egg yolks

2 teaspoons gelatin powder

1¼ cups whipped cream

*For the praline*

2 tablespoons granulated sugar

3 tablespoons whole unblanched almonds

In a heavy-bottom saucepan, combine the granulated sugar and ⅓ cup plus 1 tablespoon cold water. Stir over gentle heat until the sugar is dissolved and the water comes to a boil. Continue to boil without stirring until it turns a rich chestnut-brown color. Remove from the heat and immediately add ⅔ cup boiling water. Return to low heat and cook until the caramel thickens to a thick, syrupy texture, 4 to 6 minutes. The cooking time depends on the size of the pan and the degree of heat.

Meanwhile, in a mixing bowl, whisk the egg yolks until fluffy, then pour the boiling caramel syrup onto the egg yolks, whisking continuously until the mixture reaches the ribbon stage or holds a figure-eight shape. Put 2 tablespoons of water into a small heat-safe bowl, measure the gelatin carefully, and sprinkle it over the water. Let soak for a few minutes until the gelatin has absorbed the water and feels spongy to the touch. Sit the bowl in a saucepan of simmering water and let the gelatin dissolve completely—all the granules will dissolve and it should look perfectly clear.

Stir a few spoonfuls of the mousse into the gelatin, then carefully add the gelatin mixture to the remaining mousse. Gently fold in the whipped cream. Pour the mousse into six individual serving dishes or one larger serving dish. Cover and refrigerate until set.

To make the praline, put the sugar into a small heavy-bottom saucepan over low heat and sprinkle the almonds on top in a single layer. Do not stir. Gradually the sugar will melt and turn to a syrup. When this happens, and not before, rotate the pan so the caramel syrup coats the almonds. By now the almonds should be popping. Turn onto a nonstick baking mat or a lightly oiled baking sheet. Let cool completely and harden, then crush to a coarse powder.

Serve the mousse topped with spoonfuls of the whipped cream and decorated with the praline.

## VARIATION

*Caramel Soufflé* Fold in 2 stiffly beaten large organic, free-range egg whites after the cream. Refrigerate until set and decorate as before.

# SUMMER PUDDING

Serves 12 to 16

Summer Pudding, bursting with soft fruit and served with lots of softly whipped cream, is one of the very best desserts of the year. I actually make Summer Pudding with cake, a sort of Marie Antoinette version, but many people line the bowl with slices of white bread instead. I've used a mixture of fruit here, but it is also delicious made with black currants alone. Summer Fruit Salad with Rose Geranium (page 176) also makes a successful filling, but you need to cook the black currants and red currants until they burst and then add the soft fruit. Remember to pour the fruit and syrup while boiling hot into the sponge-lined bowl, otherwise the syrup will not soak through the sponge properly.

2 (7-inch) round sponge cakes

6 to 8 large rose geranium leaves (*Pelargonium graveolens*)

3 cups granulated sugar

3 cups cold water

2 cups black currants

2 cups red currants

2¾ cups raspberries or 1⅓ cups raspberries and 1½ cups hulled strawberries

softly whipped cream, to serve

Cut each sponge in half horizontally. Line a 1¾-quart bowl with the cake, crusty side inward. It doesn't matter if it looks quite patched, as it will blend together later.

In a stainless steel saucepan, combine the rose geranium leaves, sugar, and cold water. Bring to a boil and boil for 2 minutes. Add the black currants and red currants and cook until the fruits burst, 3 to 4 minutes. Remove from the heat and add the raspberries (and strawberries if using). Immediately ladle some of the hot liquid and fruit into the sponge-lined bowl (sit it on a plate to catch the overflow later). When about half full, place any scraps of cake in the center, then fill to the top with the fruit. Cover with a final layer of sponge. Put a plate on top and press down with a heavy weight. Let cool completely. Refrigerate for a minimum of 24 hours before serving, but it will keep for 5 to 6 days.

To serve, unmold onto a deep serving dish and pour any leftover fruit and syrup over the top and around the sides. Serve with lashings of softly whipped cream.

# CHOCOLATE MERINGUE GATEAU

Serves 6

*This recipe makes two layers of meringue, but you can double the ingredients for a celebration cake or to make individual meringues.*

2 large organic, free-range egg whites

1 cup sifted powdered sugar

2 heaping teaspoons unsweetened cocoa
   (I use Valrhona), plus more for decorating

*For the chocolate & rum cream*

1 ounce best-quality bittersweet chocolate

½ ounce unsweetened chocolate

1 tablespoon Jamaican rum

1 tablespoon heavy cream

1¼ cups softly whipped cream

*For the chocolate wafers*

2 ounces best-quality bittersweet chocolate

Preheat the oven to 300°F.

Cover a large baking sheet with parchment paper. Draw two 7½-inch circles on the paper. Ensure your mixing bowl is dry, spotlessly clean, and free of grease. Put the egg whites into the bowl and add all the powdered sugar, save 2 tablespoons, all at once. Using a handheld electric mixer, whisk until the mixture forms stiff, dry peaks. This can take 8 to 10 minutes. Sift together the cocoa and the remaining 2 tablespoons of powdered sugar, then fold in very gently. Using a palette knife, spread the meringue mixture over the drawn circles. Immediately bake for 45 minutes or until just crisp. Let cool completely, then peel off the paper.

Meanwhile, make the chocolate and rum cream: In a saucepan, very gently melt the chocolate with the rum and heavy cream, or in a heat-safe bowl set over a saucepan of barely simmering water. Let cool, then add 2 tablespoons of the whipped cream. Mix well, then fold that into the remaining whipped cream; do not stir too much or it may curdle.

Make the chocolate wafers: In a heat-safe bowl set over a saucepan of barely simmering water, melt the chocolate, stirring until smooth. Spread onto a nonstick baking mat or heavy baking sheet. Let set in a cool place until firm enough to cut into squares or diamonds.

Sandwich together the two meringue disks with most of the chocolate and rum cream and then pipe rosettes on top. Decorate with the chocolate wafers and a sprinkling of cocoa.

# BLACK CURRANT FOOL

Serves 6

Fools are super easy to make, and you can use a variety of fruit from rhubarb to green gooseberries. Raspberries and strawberries make a delicious fool also, but do not need to be cooked first.

3¼ cups fresh or frozen black currants
¾ cup plus 1 tablespoon Stock Syrup (see right)
2½ cups very softly whipped cream
granulated sugar, to taste (optional)
1 large organic, free-range egg white, beaten
   until stiff (optional)
whole milk (optional)
shortbread cookies, to serve

*For the stock syrup*
¾ cup plus 2 tablespoons granulated sugar
1¼ cups water

Make the stock syrup: In a saucepan, dissolve the sugar in the water and bring to a boil. Boil for 2 minutes, then let cool. Cover with plastic wrap and refrigerate until needed.

In a stainless steel saucepan, cover the black currants with the stock syrup. Bring to a boil and cook until the fruits burst, 4 to 5 minutes. Using a blender or food processor, blend the fruit until pureed, then pass through a strainer into a bowl. Let cool, then fold in the whipped cream. Frozen black currants tend to be less sweet, so taste and add extra sugar if needed. The stiffly beaten egg white may be added to lighten the fool, although it should not be very stiff, more like the texture of softly whipped cream. If it's too stiff, stir in a bit of milk rather than more cream. Serve with shortbread cookies.

Alternatively, layer the black currant puree and softly whipped cream in tall sundae glasses, finished with a drizzle of puree thinned with a bit of water or stock syrup over the top.

## VARIATIONS

*Black Currant Ice Cream* Leftover fool (when made with cream alone) may be frozen to make delicious ice cream. Serve with coulis made by thinning the black currant puree with a bit more water or stock syrup.

*Black Currant Popsicles* Add a bit more stock syrup and dilute with extra water if necessary. It needs to taste sweeter than you would like because the freezing process dulls the sweetness. Pour the mixture into popsicle molds, cover, insert sticks, and freeze until needed. Best eaten within a few days.

# BALLYMALOE VANILLA ICE CREAM

Serves 12 to 16

Surprise, surprise—really good cream makes really good ice cream. The Ballymaloe ice creams are made with an egg-mousse base and softly whipped cream. It produces a deliciously rich ice cream with a smooth texture that does not need additional whisking during the freezing period. This ice cream should not be served frozen hard; remove it from the freezer at least 10 minutes before serving. Other flavorings can be added to the basic recipe. Liquid ingredients such as melted chocolate or coffee should be folded into the mousse before adding the cream. For chunkier ingredients such as chocolate chips or muscatel raisins soaked in Pedro Ximénez sherry or rum, dates, or prunes, finish the ice cream, semifreeze it, and then stir them through, otherwise they will sink to the bottom.

4 large organic, free-range egg yolks (reserve the whites for making meringue)

½ cup granulated sugar

¾ cup plus 1 tablespoon cold water

seeds from ⅓ vanilla pod or 1 teaspoon pure vanilla extract

5 cups softly whipped cream (measured after it is whipped, for accuracy)

In a mixing bowl, whisk the egg yolks until light and fluffy.

In a small heavy-bottom saucepan, combine the sugar and cold water and stir over low heat until the sugar is completely dissolved. Remove the spoon and boil the syrup until it reaches the "thread" stage, about 223 to 235°F—it will look thick and syrupy, and when a metal spoon is dipped in, the last drops of syrup will form thin threads. Pour the boiling syrup in a steady stream onto the egg yolks, whisking continuously with a wire whisk. Add the vanilla seeds or vanilla extract and continue to whisk the mixture until it fluffs up into a thick, creamy white mousse.

This is the stage at which, if you're deviating from this recipe, you can add liquid flavorings such as coffee. Fold the softly whipped cream into the mousse. Pour into a stainless steel or plastic bowl, cover, and freeze.

## VARIATION

*Vanilla Ice Cream with Pedro Ximénez Raisins* Warm some Pedro Ximénez sherry. Pour over raisins and let soak to plump up and macerate, then add to the ice cream. Drizzle a bit of Pedro Ximénez over the ice cream on the plate just before you tuck in.

# MERINGUE NESTS with strawberries & cream

Serves 6

I no longer use strawberries or raspberries out of season, as they, particularly strawberries, have zero flavor and likely more exposed to pesticides and herbicides. There are many good things to fill these meringue nests with—black currants, poached kumquats, rhubarb, *fraises des bois*...

2 large organic, free-range egg whites
1 cup sifted powdered sugar
mint or lemon balm leaves, to garnish

*For the filling*
1½ cups hulled small strawberries in season
1 cup whipped cream

Preheat the oven to 300°F.

Cover a baking sheet with parchment paper. Draw four 3½-inch circles on the paper. Ensure your mixing bowl is dry, spotlessly clean, and free of grease. Put the egg whites and powdered sugar into the bowl. Using a handheld electric mixer, whisk until the mixture forms stiff, dry peaks. This can take 8 to 10 minutes.

Put the meringue mixture into a pastry bag fitted with a small star tip. Pipe a few blobs onto each circle and spread thinly with a palette knife. The meringue should not be more than ¼ inch thick. Then carefully pipe a wall of meringue rosettes around the edge of each circle.

Bake for 45 minutes or until the meringue nests will lift easily off the paper. Turn off the oven and let the meringues cool in the oven.

To assemble, slice the strawberries lengthwise. Pipe some whipped cream into each meringue nest and arrange the strawberry slices on top. Decorate with tiny rosettes of whipped cream and mint or lemon balm leaves.

## VARIATIONS

⌐ *Meringue Nests with Fall Raspberries & Pistachios* Substitute raspberries for strawberries, scatter with chopped pistachios, and decorate with mint leaves.

⌐ *Meringue Nests with Lemon Curd* Substitute homemade lemon curd for the strawberries and decorate with mint leaves.

# SUMMER FRUIT SALAD with rose geranium

Serves 8 to 10

Rose geranium (*Pelargonium graveolens*) and many other varieties of scented geraniums are ever present on our windowsills here at Ballymaloe. We use the delicious lemon-scented leaves in all sorts of ways. Occasionally we use the pretty purple flowers as well to enliven and add magic to otherwise simple dishes. The crystallized leaves, all frosty and crinkly, are wonderful with fresh cream cheese and fat, juicy blackberries. I discovered this recipe, which has now become a perennial favorite, quite by accident a few summers ago as I raced to make a dessert in a hurry with the ingredients I had on hand.

⅔ cup raspberries

⅔ cup loganberries

1 cup red currants

1 cup black currants

¾ cup hulled small strawberries

¾ cup blueberries

¾ cup *fraises des bois* or wild strawberries

¾ cup blackberries

*For the syrup*

1¾ cups plus 2 tablespoons cold water

1⅔ cups granulated sugar

6 to 8 large rose geranium leaves, plus more
    to decorate

In a white china or glass bowl, combine all the fresh berries. In a stainless steel saucepan, combine the cold water, sugar, and rose geranium leaves. Bring slowly to a boil, stirring until the sugar dissolves. Boil for just 2 minutes. Let cool for 10 to 15 minutes or more, then pour the syrup over the berries and set aside to macerate for several hours, if you have time.

Remove the geranium leaves. Serve the fruit salad chilled on its own, or with softly whipped cream or vanilla ice cream (page 174). Decorate with a few fresh rose geranium leaves.

## VARIATION

⌒ *Winter Fruit Salad with Sweet Geranium Leaves* Follow the recipe above but substitute best-quality frozen berries and currants. Pour the boiling syrup over the berries in the bowl. This will thaw the fruit and cool the syrup at the same time.

# CRÈME CARAMEL with caramel shards

*A timeless dessert that is exquisite when carefully made—serve chilled.*

*For the custard*
1½ cups whole milk
vanilla pod or ½ teaspoon pure vanilla
   extract (optional)
4 large organic, free-range eggs
3 tablespoons superfine sugar

*For the caramel syrup*
1 cup granulated sugar
⅓ cup plus 2 tablespoons water
*For the caramel sauce*
¼ cup water
*For the caramel shards*
⅔ to ¾ cup granulated sugar

Preheat the oven to 300°F. Put the cold milk into a saucepan and add the vanilla pod, if using. Bring to just under boiling point. Let cool and infuse for 10 to 15 minutes. Whether you are using a vanilla pod or vanilla extract, the milk must be brought to just under boiling point first. In a mixing bowl, whisk the eggs, superfine sugar, and vanilla extract, if using, until well mixed but not too fluffy.

Meanwhile, make the caramel syrup: In a heavy-bottom saucepan, combine the sugar and water and stir over gentle heat until the sugar is fully dissolved. Bring to a boil, remove the spoon, and boil until the caramel syrup becomes dark golden brown or what we term chestnut color. Do not stir or shake the pan. When the caramel syrup is ready for lining the molds, it must be used immediately or it will become hard and cold. Coat the bottom of six 3-inch soufflé dishes or cups with the hot caramel syrup. Dilute the remaining caramel syrup with the ¼ cup of water, return to the heat to dissolve, and set aside.

Pour the slightly cooled milk onto the egg mixture, whisking gently as you pour. Strain and pour into the prepared molds, filling them to the top. Place the molds in a bain-marie—a roasting pan filled with enough hot water to come halfway up the sides of the molds. Cover with a sheet of parchment paper and bake for about 35 minutes. Test the custard for doneness by inserting a toothpick into the center, which will come out clean when the custard is fully cooked.

Meanwhile, make the caramel shards: Put the sugar into a shallow stainless steel saucepan and stir continuously over medium heat until it melts and caramelizes. When it has almost reached the "chestnut" stage, remove from the heat and let stand for a few minutes. Spoon onto an oiled baking sheet or silicone paper. Let set until cold and crisp, then break into shards.

Let the caramels cool, then turn out onto individual plates and pour the caramel sauce around the edge. Decorate with the caramel shards.

# COUNTRY RHUBARB CAKE

Serves 8

This traditional rhubarb cake, based on an enriched bread dough, was made all over Ireland and is a treasured memory from my childhood. It would have originally been baked in the bastible or "baker" over the open fire. My mother, who taught me this recipe, varied the filling with the seasons—first rhubarb, then gooseberries, and later in the fall, apples and plums.

2¾ cups all-purpose flour

pinch of salt

½ teaspoon baking soda

¼ cup superfine sugar, plus more for sprinkling

6 tablespoons (¾ stick) butter

1 large organic, free-range egg

⅔ cup whole milk, buttermilk, or sour milk

1½ pounds rhubarb, trimmed and finely chopped

¾ cup plus 2 tablespoons to 1 cup plus
  2 tablespoons granulated sugar

beaten organic, free-range egg, to glaze

softly whipped cream and brown sugar,
  to serve

Preheat the oven to 350°F.

Sift the flour, salt, and baking soda into a mixing bowl and stir in the sugar. Cut the butter into the dry mixture using a pastry cutter or by pinching the fat into the mixture with your fingertips. In a small bowl, beat together the egg and milk, buttermilk, or sour milk. Make a hollow in the center of the dough mixture. Pour in most of the liquid and mix to a soft dough, then add the remaining liquid if necessary.

Turn out the soft dough onto a lightly floured work surface and pat gently into a circle. Divide into two pieces, one slightly larger than the other; reserve the larger one for the lid.

Dip your fingers in flour. Roll out the smaller piece of dough and use to line a 10-inch enamel or Pyrex pie plate. Scatter the rhubarb all over the bottom and sprinkle with the granulated sugar. Brush the edges of the dough with the beaten egg. Roll out the other piece of dough until it is exactly the size to cover the plate, lift it on, and press the edges gently to seal them. Do not worry if you have to patch the soft dough. Press the edges together lightly with the tines of a fork and make a hole in the center for the steam to escape. Brush again with beaten egg and sprinkle with a very small amount of superfine sugar.

Bake for 45 minutes to 1 hour or until the rhubarb is soft and the crust is golden. Let sit for 10 to 15 minutes before serving so the juice can soak into the crust. Sprinkle with superfine sugar. Serve while warm with a bowl of softly whipped cream and some moist brown sugar.

# BALLYMALOE COFFEE ICE CREAM
with Irish coffee sauce

Serves 6 to 8

This ice cream is so good! You may be surprised that I am using instant coffee, but believe me it works brilliantly here—liquid espresso will result in splinters of ice. It will keep for months in the freezer but is much more fresh-tasting when eaten within a couple of days of being made.

*For the coffee ice cream*

2 organic, free-range egg yolks

¼ cup granulated sugar

⅓ cup plus 2 tablespoons cold water

½ teaspoon vanilla extract

3 teaspoons instant coffee granules

½ teaspoon boiling water

2½ cups whipped cream

*For the Irish coffee sauce*

¾ cup plus 2 tablespoons granulated sugar

⅓ cup water

1 cup strong coffee or espresso

1 tablespoon Irish whiskey

Make the ice cream: In a mixing bowl, whisk the egg yolks until light and fluffy.

In a small heavy-bottom saucepan, combine the sugar and cold water and stir over low heat until the sugar is completely dissolved. Remove the spoon and boil the syrup until it reaches the "thread" stage, about 223 to 235°F—it will look thick and syrupy, and when a metal spoon is dipped in, the last drops of syrup will form thin threads. Pour the boiling syrup in a steady stream onto the egg yolks, whisking continuously with a wire whisk. Continue to whisk the mixture until it fluffs up into a thick, creamy white mousse that will hold a figure eight. Stir in the vanilla extract.

In a small bowl, mix the instant coffee with the boiling water. Add some of the mousse to the coffee paste, then fold the coffee mixture into the remaining mousse. Carefully fold in the softly whipped cream. Pour into a stainless steel or plastic bowl, cover, and freeze.

Make the Irish coffee sauce: In a heavy-bottom saucepan, combine the sugar and water and stir over medium heat until the sugar dissolves and the water comes to a boil. Remove the spoon and do not stir again until the syrup turns a pale golden color. Then add the coffee and return to the heat to dissolve. Let cool and add the whiskey. This sauce keeps brilliantly for 2 to 3 months and doesn't need to be refrigerated.

To serve, scoop the ice cream into individual bowls and pour the sauce over the top.

# GREEN GOOSEBERRY COMPOTE with elderflowers

Serves 6 to 8

When I'm driving through country lanes in late May or early June, I suddenly spy the elderflower blossoms in the hedgerows. I know then it's time to go and search on gooseberry bushes for the first hard, green fruit, far too underripe at that stage to eat raw, but wonderful cooked in tarts or fools, or in this delicious compote. Elderflowers have an extraordinary affinity with green gooseberries and by a happy arrangement of nature they are both in season at the same time.

2 pounds green gooseberries

2 to 3 elderflower heads

2 cups granulated sugar

2½ cups cold water

elderflowers, to decorate

elderflower cream (see method), to serve

Remove the blossom and stem ends from the gooseberries. Tie the elderflower heads in a small square of cheesecloth (alternatively, just add them whole and fish them out later), put into a stainless steel or enameled saucepan, add the sugar, and cover with the cold water. Bring slowly to a boil and continue to boil for 2 minutes. Add the gooseberries and simmer just until the fruits burst. (The tart green gooseberries must actually burst, otherwise the compote will be too bitter.) Let cool completely.

Serve in a pretty bowl and decorate with fresh elderflowers. Serve with elderflower cream (whipped cream flavored with elderflower cordial).

## VARIATION

*Green Gooseberry & Elderflower Fool* Using a blender or food processor, blend the compote until pureed, then mix with softly whipped cream to taste—about half volume of whipped cream to fruit puree. Serve chilled with shortbread cookies.

# APPLE CHARLOTTE

Serves 4 to 6

This is the scrummiest, most wickedly rich apple pudding ever. A friend, Peter Lamb, makes it as a special treat for me every now and then. It's also a brilliant and delicious way to use up bread and apples. I make my Apple Charlotte from old varieties of apples —my favorites are Egremont Russet, Charles Ross, Cox's Orange Pippin, or Pitmaston Pineapple. It's sinfully rich but gorgeous.

1 cup (2 sticks) butter

2¼ pounds apples, preferably heirloom

2 to 3 tablespoons water

¾ cup plus 2 tablespoons superfine sugar, plus
   more for sprinkling

2 large organic, free-range egg yolks

good-quality white bread

softly whipped cream, to serve

Preheat the oven to 400°F.

Make the clarified butter: In a saucepan, melt the butter gently. Remove from the heat and let it sit for a few minutes, then spoon the crusty white layer of salt particles off the top of the melted butter. Underneath this crust there is clear liquid butter, which is the clarified butter. The milky liquid at the bottom can be discarded or used in a white sauce. Clarified butter is excellent for cooking because it can withstand a higher temperature when the salt and milk particles are removed. It will keep, covered, in the refrigerator for several weeks.

Peel and core the apples. In a stainless steel saucepan, melt a bit of the clarified butter. Chop the apples into cubes and add to the pan with the water and sugar. Cover and cook over gentle heat until the apples break down into a thick pulp. Beat in the egg yolks one by one—this helps to enrich and thicken the apple puree. Taste and add a bit more sugar if necessary.

Melt the remaining clarified butter and use a small amount to brush the inside of a 5 x 8-inch loaf pan, then sprinkle with superfine sugar. Cut the crusts off the bread and cut into strips about 5 inches long and 1½ inches wide. Quickly brush with the clarified butter. Line the sides of the pan with the butter-soaked bread. Cut another strip to fit tightly into the bottom of the pan. Brush on both sides with butter and tuck in tightly. Fill the center with the apple. Cut another strip of bread to fit the top. Brush with melted butter on both sides and fit it neatly to cover the puree.

Bake for 20 minutes, then reduce the heat to 350°F and bake for another 15 minutes or until the bread is crisp and a rich golden color.

To serve, run a knife around the edges in case the bread has stuck to the pan. Invert onto a warm oval serving plate. It won't look like a thing of beauty, as it may collapse a bit, but it will taste wonderful. Serve with lots of softly whipped cream.

# LEMON FLUFF with limoncello cream

This is a gorgeous old-fashioned family dessert that separates into two quite distinct layers when it cooks—it has a lovely fluffy top and a creamy lemon base, provided it is not overcooked.

3 tablespoons butter, softened

1 cup plus 2 tablespoons superfine sugar

3 large organic, free-range eggs

½ cup plus 1½ tablespoons all-purpose flour

2 organic lemons

1¼ cups whole milk

powdered sugar, to decorate

1¼ cups softly whipped cream flavored with limoncello, or crème fraiche, to serve

Preheat the oven to 350°F.

In a mixing bowl, cream the butter until really soft, then add the superfine sugar and beat well. Separate the egg yolks and beat in one by one, then stir in the flour.

Using the finest part of a stainless steel grater, grate the zest of both lemons. Squeeze and strain the juice. Add the grated zest and juice to the batter, then stir in the milk.

In a mixing bowl, whisk the egg whites until stiff, then gently fold into the lemon batter. Pour into individual baking dishes or small ramekins or a 1¼-quart pie dish and place in a bain-marie—a roasting pan filled with enough hot water to come halfway up the sides of the dishes or dish. Bake for 35 to 40 minutes.

Dredge with powdered sugar and serve right away alongside the softly whipped cream flavored to taste with limoncello, or some crème fraiche.

## ACKNOWLEDGMENTS

I've been so touched by the many people for whom the *Simply Delicious* cookbooks hold a special memory.

Those who bring me well-worn, gravy splattered copies to sign. This book is for all of you who requested a reprint. I've chosen my 100 favorite recipes from *Simply Delicious 1, 2, Fish,* and *Vegetables* —what a tough choice that was and such a revelation that so many recipes have stood the test of time and are still simply delicious.

Special thanks to Joanna Copestick for commissioning this collection and my editor Vicky Orchard for keeping me in check, no easy matter…To photographer Pete Cassidy for the beautiful photos and food stylist Lizzie Harris and prop stylist Agathe Gits for cooking and styling my food so beautifully.

Rosalie Dunne, my heroic PA of 24 years, came out of retirement to type the manuscript. Can you imagine that I still write all my books in longhand 29 years later? Thank you Rosalie.

Special thanks also to Tim and all my extended family of children, grandchildren, and once again to the recently deceased Myrtle Allen—my lifelong inspiration.